Output and Performance Measurement in Government

The State of the Art

Books of related interest

The Use of Performance Indicators in Higher Education:
A Critical Analysis of Developing Practice   2nd edition
Martin Cave, Stephen Hanney, and Maurice Kogan
ISBN 1 85302 518 6

Evaluating Higher Education
Edited by Maurice Kogan
ISBN 1 85302 510 0

Evaluation as Policymaking:
Introducing Evaluation into a National Decentralised Educational System
Edited by Marit Granheim, Maurice Kogan and Ulf Lundgren
ISBN 1 85302 515 1

Directors of Education - Facing Reform
Tony Bush, Maurice Kogan and Tony Lenney
ISBN 1 85302 506 2

Evaluation   2nd edition
Edited by Joyce Lishman
ISBN 1 85302 006 0

Performance Review in Social Work Agencies
John Tibbitt and David Pia
ISBN 1 85302 017 6

Output and Performance Measurement in Government

The State of the Art

Edited by Martin Cave, Maurice Kogan and Robert Smith

Jessica Kingsley Publishers
London

Acknowledgements
The editors are grateful to Sally Harris of Brunel University for organising the production of the manuscript and to John Evans at the Civil Service College for indispensable help with the conference on which the present book is based.

First published in 1990 by
Jessica Kingsley Publishers Ltd
118 Pentonville Road
London N1 9JN

British Library Cataloguing in Publication Data
Output and performance measurement in government : the state
    of the art.
    1. Great Britain. Government Performance. Measurement
    I. Cave, Martin II. Kogan, Maurice III. Smith, Robert
    345.41

    ISBN 1-85302-521-6

Printed and bound in Great Britain by
Biddles Ltd, Guildford and King's Lynn

Contents

Part I

The Background

Chapter 1

Introduction

Martin Cave, Maurice Kogan and Robert Smith

In November 1989, Brunel University's Centre for the Evaluation of
Public Policy and Practice (CEPPP) and the Civil Service College jointly
organised a conference on output and performance measurement in
Government. This volume contains revised versions of the papers
presented there, as well as some additional material.

Output and performance measurement was undoubtedly one of the
growth industries of the 1980s. A quick glance through the pages of the
Public Expenditure White Papers of the latter half of the decade will show
the expansion in the scale of output and performance measurement; there
were about 1200 in 1986 and 2300 in 1989. The main impetus for this
growth was the 1982 White Paper on *Efficiency and Effectiveness in the
Civil Service* (Cmnd 2616). The aims of the Financial Management
Initiative announced in that document were to:

'Promote in each department and organisation a system in which
managers at all levels have

- a clear view of their objectives, and means to assess and,
  wherever possible, measure, outputs or performance in relation
  to those objectives;

- well-defined responsibility for making the best use of their
  resources, including a critical scrutiny of output and value for
  money;

- the information (particularly about costs), the training and the
  access to expert advice which they need to exercise their
  responsibilities effectively.'

There has been little argument with the basic proposition that it is sensible
and helpful to try to set clear objectives. Work is better organised and
more effective if people know what they are trying to achieve and what

their priorities should be. Likewise there are few people in the public sector who would disagree with the proposition that, if objectives are clear, it is helpful to compare actual performance with intended performance. Such comparisons enable effort to be redirected if performance is not what it should be and help to increase the probability of ultimate success. Where there has been concern about the requirement to set clear objectives and measure performance, it is normally concern about how to carry out these tasks in practice.

The practical difficulties arise in part from the nature of the work in some areas of Government. It is often said that objectives and performance measures are much more straightforward in the private sector. There the bottom line is clear; ultimately a company has to make an acceptable profit, and units and individuals within a company are all judged by their contribution to that overriding objective. This is certainly an over-simplification. Many elements of a company's strategy will contain elements of subjectivity - for example consumer perceptions of the quality of the product, staff commitment, the contribution of support departments such as personnel, finance and research, and the work of many individuals who are not themselves heading a cost or profit centre. Nevertheless, outputs are generally more easily identified and the ultimate requirement for a reasonable profit provides at least a clear focus and starting point.

In the public sector, there are perhaps more areas of work with similarities to trading organisations than has generally been recognised. Indeed, this is one of the main thrusts of the 'Next Steps' initiative announced in February 1988 and a reason for the introduction of Executive Agencies (see *Improving Management in Government: The Next Steps*, Efficiency Unit.) Often there is a need for greater attention to quality of output and customer service, and levels of service quality cannot be adequately proxied by physical output measures. It is necessary to try to measure quality of service directly despite all the difficulties, which often include lack of agreement on what the elements of good service are.

This difficulty arises because many public sector organisations are trying to serve the whole community, or at least to serve a wide range of people with different wishes and expectations. Central Government departments in particular cover a wide range of activities and responsibilities: the Department of the Environment, discussed in Chapter 9 below, provides an excellent example of this.

Thus the public sector frequently faces the problems of measuring output in difficult areas where quality of output is important, of meeting subjective final needs, and of covering a wide range of work within a single operating unit. Often attempts to measure output and performance take the investigator into uncharted waters. But while the difficulty of identifying adequate performance measures and indicators should not be underestimated, significant progress has been made in the past five or ten years. Substantial experience has already been gained but further development, sharing of experience and critical review of the issues are all fully possible. There are no easy formulae which can be widely applied; it is doubtful whether anyone could ever produce a standard guidebook to performance measurement for the whole of the public sector. Each area of activity has to be tackled individually, and this involves difficult, fundamental thinking about ultimate purposes and key priorities. Nevertheless, the experience and thoughts of others can offer insights and suggest particular approaches which may be helpful.

The conference which has led to this volume was arranged with this exchange of experience in mind. It was designed to aid those who recognise the value of performance measures and are actively seeking to develop measures which will help managers to manage more effectively. The contributors were chosen to provide a mixture of practitioners and academics. Practitioners who are taking the lead in the development of indicators report what has actually been achieved, and describe the practical difficulties. The academics take a more detached view (except, perhaps inevitably, in the case of indicators for higher education), review progress and identify issues common to a whole range of activities. The editors have sought to maintain the flavour of the conference presentations - some broad overviews, some detailed analyses.

The book starts with reviews of the policy background and of the range of techniques, concepts and approaches which can be employed in a number of sectors. It then shows examples of work done in particular sectors, returning finally to the general issues in order to forecast what lies ahead.

Peter Hennessy's introductory paper sets the wider scene, pointing out the potential value, and limitations, of performance measurement in the wider political context. Michael Barrow continues the scene-setting in the technical arena, by clarifying the concepts of technical and allocative inefficiency, the circumstances under which they can be measured, approaches to their measurement, and the ambiguities which arise in interpreting the results.

Sue Lewis and Jeff Jones then look at the current situation in Government departments, surveying the background, terminology, classification and uses of performance measures and indicators. They consider some of the difficulties encountered in the development and effective use of the measures.

That leads into the first of the sector studies, a review of performance indicators for higher education and research by Martin Cave and Stephen Hanney. Their chapter looks first at frameworks and models relevant to the measurement of performance in these areas, and then reports on the development of performance indicators in the United Kingdom. After considering the indicators currently in use it reviews the impact and forecasts their impact on management, resource allocation and behaviour.

The sectoral study of health services by Helen Roberts reports progress made in three areas:

(a) medical audit, which looks at medical processes, the treatments chosen and their results, and at patient satisfaction;

(b) assessing outcomes, ultimately mortality and the quality of life following treatment;

(c) the performance indicators produced and used currently in the Health Service.

Two chapters on local government follow. The first is contributed by David Henderson-Stewart of the Audit Commission. He describes the need for performance analysis, and proposes some approaches which can be adopted to obtain indicators of quality and effectiveness. He suggests that effective performance review depends on accountable management, commitment to quality, and proper reporting procedures. David Burningham then discusses how performance indicators can affect behaviour and management styles in local authorities.

The final sectoral study by Peter Daffern and Grahame Walshe concentrates first on how to measure the aggregate efficiency of a central Government department and takes the Department of the Environment as an example. As well as considering measures of output productivity in central administration, the chapter gives examples of performance measures used for some programme expenditure and for some of the DOE's non-departmental public bodies.

An overview by Christopher Pollitt looks back over the development of performance indicators and suggests that in some respects they have not yet developed strong enough roots. Not enough people fully understand and actively use them. He concludes by suggesting they can be encouraged to develop more strongly. Finally, a concluding chapter by Martin Cave and Maurice Kogan reviews the lessons of the book and looks forward to future developments.

The editors hope that the chapters presented here, which bring together a range of experience, will be helpful in providing new insights and encouragement to all who are actively seeking to develop and improve performance measurement in the public services. Having clearly set out our objectives, we shall, in the spirit of the volume, try to monitor how well they have been achieved.

Chapter 2

The Political and Administrative Background

Peter Hennessy

At conferences like this you have to begin with a health warning. It is one the great Harold MacMillan gave in 1949 (he was always ahead of the field). He said 'we have not overcome the divine right of kings to succumb before the divine right of the expert'. You have to watch that, I think, on days like this in particular. So I have decided my self-appointed task is to be an antidote to the hyper-technical and the over-sophisticated. There is a good reason for that - I am incapable of doing anything else.

The subject of your discussion matters to everybody, not just to the technicians of state. I tell you why I think this is. It is because, as Clive Priestley, first chief-of-staff in the Government's Rayner Efficiency Unit, put it, there has been a huge philosophical gap both in political science and political philosophy and in management thinking in this country. Priestley, in his 19th century way, described the missing element as the philosophy of 'the well-managed state'. The British state got big without anybody thinking about it. Until the 'Next Steps' proposals in 1988 for independent Executive Agencies, for example, nobody had really thought about the ancient notion of ministerial responsibility which was dreamed up in the days when it could work in the early nineteenth century, when the Board of Trade consisted of two ministers and 20 clerks. The model of the minister being answerable for everything - in fact being capable of knowing everything - was busted by the time of the Labour Exchanges in 1909 and certainly by the time the National Insurance Commission was established in 1911.

Very few people have thought about this. It is partly to do with the British obsession with, or aversion from, writing down anything that matters, whether it be the powers of the Monarch or the nature of British Constitution. I have only found the latter set down in one place and that is in the Central Office of Information handbook called *Britain* which is written each year very slowly in English for foreigners. It was in 1947 - the Festival of Britain year - that they decided they would write down what the British constitution was, and as far as I know that is the only time the Crown servants ever dared to do it. It is worth looking at. It does not tell you anything but it is the only place we have it written down. This theme of mine, the philosophy of the well-managed state (or absence thereof) in this country, is absolutely crucial given the size of the British state, the amount of money that passes through its hands, and its indispensability for the life chances of 56 million of us. But, like all big issues, we shy away from it and we spend all our time nitpicking.

Turning now to the management developments in the 1980s, I was initially as sceptical as everybody else, given that most of us had lived through so many Civil Service reforms that we were incapable of believing that any of them could be beneficial. I succumbed to that well known disease of the Under-Secretary (a version of the law of unintended consequences) - that any change will be for the worst. But I have to say that I was wrong, and I was wrong in many ways.

The first area in which I was wrong was to think that the Rayner philosophy of efficiency in Government, as it was known in the early days, was essentially a crude tool for bashing the public service and cutting manpower. I came to think from 1980-81 onwards that if you were of a centre-leftist position (which I was and still am), there was a great deal in it for a future Government whatever its political coloration. For example, take Michael Heseltine's MINIS programme for supplying management information for the Department of the Environment. When he had a little press conference of the five journalists who were interested in this in 1980-81, it suddenly occurred to me (and, in fact, he concurred with this when I put it to him) that it was as useful a tool for a Labour Secretary of State of the Environment keen on expanding State activity as it was for him who was trying to trim the 66 directorates that the DoE then had. And the reason for this is that it is surely not in the interest of any Secretary of State, whatever level of state activity they want to encourage, to deploy one more pound of taxpayer's money or one more public servant than is needed on the tasks in hand as there are always plenty of demands on public resources. In other words, the MINIS side of life and its developments through the FMI should be just as useful, if not more useful, an instrument for a future Labour Government as they have been to the present administration.

Many of these reforms fell into the classic Northcote-Trevelyan mould of being politically neutral and of being a technology that was transferable from one administration to another. I only hope that proves to be the case in the 1990s if and when a change of Government takes place. Equally powerful in me is the belief that we have wasted, in this country uniquely, masses of nervous energy and time over that fruitless debate about the boundary between the public and private sector. What the Curzon Line is or was for the Poles, the boundary between the public and private has become to us. It has dominated the political debate in all our lifetimes.

Almost a secondary question, given the theological nature of this debate, has been the effective delivery of services. We have an ability to shudder at the thought of state power in a way that the French never have (nor do most of the Western Europeans) and it has been reflected, as I say, in the extraordinarily crude debate between the two major political parties which still continues. Now one of the reasons I am a 'Next Steps' man is, I think, that at last there is a chance for that crude, useless and time-wasting debate to wither away. Any effort is worthwhile to find (as I think there can be found) some kind of third way between the public and private with the virtues of both: the public sector virtues of probity, equity of treatment and a high degree of institutionalised altruism and the best of private sector - its management of resources and greater flexibility in the use of people and money. And I am very pleased that Peter Kemp, the Project Manager for the 'Next Steps' initiative, spends so much time on the conference circuit trying to put flesh on the bones of his new third force philosophy, as he calls it.

That is why today's subject matters, not just to the technicians of state but to every recipient of state service. I have never ceased to believe, in my old fashioned way, that public money can be creative money. One of the more absurd notions of the 1980s is that public money is dead money by definition. I was very struck, when Stuart Maclure published his excellent study of the school building programme that the Ministry of Education set in train after the war, by a remark of Sir Anthony Part - that in those days people still believed in the possibility of the creative public sector. In the context of 1984, when that book was published, this was a mixture of 'Down Your Way' nostalgia and heresy. I think we have suffered from that notion - of public money as dead money - as in fact we have suffered from many notions in the 1980s.

Let us give the Government credit where credit is due, and not just on the MINIS or 'Next Steps' side of things. I have been looking recently at the changes in the quality of the information contained in the Public Expenditure White Papers. When I first had to look at them in the mid-1970s you needed to have the actuarial skills of a Beveridge and the analytical horse power of a Keynes to make any sense of most of it, and the Estimates were even worse. An extraordinary degree of effort went into producing institutionalised incomprehension. It is not just because I am, like most of the British population, relatively innumerate. Even the numerate found problems with it, and remember the wonderful running story of the old Commons Expenditure Committee when its adviser, Wynne Godley, who can add up and does understand about politics and Whitehall, discovered the lost five billion pounds between forecasts and out-turn in public expenditure. From those days until now there has literally been a transformation - there is no other way of describing it.

Much of this is due to the project that Andrew Likierman and Joel Barnett started in 1983 to improve the quality of financial information and reporting in central government. Their report was good and timely when it appeared in 1984 and the degree to which the Commons Treasury and Civil Service Committee took it up was highly fortunate indeed. It is far better in our society if an all-party committee of MPs, albeit on the basis of other people's intellectual R and D, makes the running on an issue like this. And it is to the great credit of the Government and the Treasury in particular that they took up most of it. If you look at the quality difference between even mid-1980s Public Expenditure White Papers and the present ones with 2000 performance indicators written into them, and the much better presentation in their departmental booklets, you do see an extraordinary change.

For example, the Department of the Environment published its first annual report in 1983. It was a good step forward but it was essentially backward looking and had the nature of an audit. If you contrast that with the Department of Transport's chapter in the last Public Expenditure White Paper, there is no comparison, not just in the DT's forward look at current policies but in the candour of, for example, some of the charts showing the degree to which the maintenance of local roads, trunk roads and motorways has fallen behind.

I have spent most of my professional lifetime whingeing about the Whitehall's obsession with secrecy and the embarrassment-avoidance culture on which it is built. I have to admit that if you take for example the Department of Transport (which is highly politically sensitive now), the quality of its information and its honesty are breathtaking. Now you may say this is only by past Whitehall standards, and bearing in mind our position as a world leader in administrative secrecy. Even allowing for my professional whingeing in which I still indulge on the side, there has been a dramatic change. It is all to the good and it has been done in a bipartisan fashion. It does show that, even in the awful 1980s, well intentioned and capable outsiders can find allies in the Parliamentary system in an all-party, non-partisan fashion whose thinking can find real echoes inside the Treasury; and this produces practical results for all of us.

Now that is a virtuous circle, the like of which I think we have all too often forgotten about. We no longer live in a world where Royal Commissions are ever thought to be useful in any degree. We also do live in a relatively evidence-free political climate where reason is not at a high premium any more, and conviction is all. When you find a minor triumph like this, it is a moment to be savoured and time to give credit where credit it is due.

We all know that some things, though, are not susceptible to performance measurement however sophisticated it may be, however well it develops; for example, peace. The things that matter, the big things, can never be measured. I remember a conference on public administration at York in 1981 for which Chris Painter of the Birmingham Polytechnic very bravely wrote a paper on Civil Service morale in what was a very grim period in the early 1980s. Those wretched social scientists there gave him a terrible time because you cannot measure morale and you know what social scientists are like in this country; if you cannot measure it it does not exist. I have never forgotten that.

The other classic example (when you think about it) is the private performance indicator for NATO. General Ismay, the first Secretary General of NATO, invented it when he came back in 1950 to talk to the backbench Conservative defence group (who, being Empire men, were not at all familiar with notions of collective security). He was having a terrible time persuading them what NATO was really about. He said it really comes down to this, 'NATO exists for three reasons - to keep the Russians out, the Americans in and the Germans down'. Now that is the basis for a wonderful performance indicator. It has got everything (nobody can do the same for the European Economic Community, which is one reason we have all this trouble with it) and, let us be fair to NATO, it worked. The Americans have stayed in, the Russians have kept out and the Germans (so far, fingers crossed) have been kept down. That performance indicator has worked over 40 years. But there again there is no control group possible in this. You cannot actually say, 'well, we'll leave a bit of the central front undefended to see if the bastards do come through'. It is not like that. Mercifully the 175 divisions that Stalin at one point had against our six actually stayed there.

The same applies to the absence of performance indicators on the large scale for the National Health Service. We all know, or some of the older of us do, of the amount of avoidable pain and grief that our fellow countrymen and women suffered before the Emergency Hospital Service, which was the forerunner of the NHS, came into being in 1939. We can only imagine what might have been in terms of avoidable pain and suffering for our fellow countrymen but for 5 July 1948 when the NHS came into being. Everybody knows it is huge but everybody knows it is immeasurable. One of the things, I think, we have lost - that social scientists have lost - is the ability to measure such effects. Take Richard Titmuss' 1949 volume, *Problems of Social Policy*. I recommend you to get it and read his chapter on 'The Arithmetic of Stress'. What he tried to do in that (and he did it very well) was to measure the number of deaths and tragedies that occurred because of the war that you would not normally think of. For example, the number of children that were smothered in bed because they had to be rushed down into air-raid shelters or the number of children who drowned in static water tanks, kept for Civil Defence purposes. Titmuss covered a whole range of things which only somebody as sensitive as he would have thought of and would have thought of ways of measuring. That chapter is quite short but I have never seen anything like it reproduced in terms of quality or imagination since.

Conducting an overall performance assessment for a great institution like the NHS is extremely difficult. I know this from personal experience having tried to do it for the Civil Service in my book on Whitehall (Hennessy, 1989). Even when you break it up into separate chunks of policy/administration (as I did with inner cities and nuclear weapons) the problems remain daunting even when one is dealing with activities that have a tangible result.

This brings me to one or two crucial wider matters which, again, cannot be measured but which I reckon are absolutely crucial to the citizen, the quality of public services and to the calibre of the Civil Service itself. These are areas in which only failure can be measured because you only know you have got a problem when it does not work. There are three of them. One is corruption, where you only know you have got a problem when a Poulson has a bankruptcy charge brought against him, and becomes exposed. Now I think that as public services go in the world, we have more built-in barriers against corruption than anybody else, and that is a pearl beyond price. It is taken for granted and it should not be. When you look at the 160 nations recognised as such in the United Nations, only about 20 to 25 have public services of which you could really say, with hand on heart, that they are not corrupt to any institutionalised degree.

The second is deception. By and large the British public service is not in the business of deliberate deception. People take great pride in getting through 20 to 25 years in the civil service with only putting up the minimum of information required to avoid accusations of lying in Parliamentary written answers. But that really is still pretty good when you consider what most governments try and do to their citizens in most parts of the world. The moment we start slipping on that we are in real trouble.

The third one is relevant in the context of the need for the Security Service Act just passed. It is this: that no Crown servant in this country, provided the electoral systems remains clean and decent to the extent that we have elections at least once every five years in peacetime, can be in the business of subversion either on the grand scale or on a minor scale. These are the things that do matter to the quality of the public service on a vast scale, and yet they are not susceptible to measurement and you can only know when it is going wrong and even then it is very hard to pin it down. These areas are very, very difficult but they are all too serious to be left to the Civil Service Pay and Conditions of Service Code and that ludicrously inadequate memorandum which Robert Armstrong sent round after the Ponting affair. For me, these are key indicators of constitutional health as well as day to day performance by the public service, and here no FMI and no 'Next Steps' can help. I have always felt that if ever we did hit really serious trouble in this country on any of these fronts - corruption, deception, subversion - some people would resign and make it plain that there was wrongdoing even though they are not allowed to do that under the Armstrong memorandum (according to which you can complain up and down the line, you can take it to the Head of Profession and then you can resign, but you cannot tell anybody). But I like to think that some people would resign and speak out rather than collaborate or go along with that.

Now if this indicator of mind, this performance indicator which matters terribly to me, is ever put to the test I should be very surprised, but if it is and I am wrong, I would lay down my pen forever; I simply would not write another word about Whitehall. Some of you might think, that to achieve that result, it would be cheap at the price.

Reference

Hennessy, P., (1989 and 1990), *Whitehall*, Secker and Warburg, New York: Fontana, London.

Chapter 3

Techniques of Efficiency Measurement in the Public Sector

Michael M Barrow

Introduction

Efficiency measurement in the public sector has been the subject of much recent research, at both theoretical and empirical levels. The present government's concern to improve efficiency in the public sector has been the spur to many empirical studies, and this in turn has led to an examination of the logical underpinnings of existing indicators and to the search for better ones.

This chapter provides a brief outline of the theoretical work which has been undertaken on performance measurement and draws some lessons for the practical application and interpretation of performance indicators. These arguments are illustrated by reference to the performance of local education authorities (LEAs) in England.

The case is made in favour of a formal approach to the problem of efficiency measurement, even if performance measurement is ultimately carried out in a more informal or *ad hoc* manner in practice. This approach will aid interpretation of any results obtained, for it will help the researcher be aware of the shortcomings of the results.

In order to focus attention upon issues of measurement and estimation, the chapter abstracts from many of the problems associated with performance indicators, such as those relating to the measurement of quality as well as quantity of output. This is not to deny the importance of these neglected aspects which are considered in other sections of our book. A more detailed account of some of the techniques described here can be found in Barrow and Wagstaffe (1989).

Technical and Allocative Efficiency

The examination of efficiency in a theoretical framework begins with the familiar economic concepts of cost and production functions. Inefficiency in producing output then manifests itself in two possible ways: by output being less than the maximum level attainable given the level of inputs available, or because the wrong input proportions have been chosen to produce the output. Either of these will result in the cost of producing the output being higher than the feasible minimum. The first type of inefficiency is known as technical inefficiency, the latter is known as allocative or price inefficiency, since inputs are not being used such that the ratio of marginal products equals the ratio of factor prices. We do not deal here with another type of allocative efficiency, when either too much or too little output is produced.

These concepts may usefully be presented in an isoquant diagram, as in Figure 3.1. Two inputs, x_1 and x_2, are used to produce output Y. For simplicity of exposition constant returns to scale are assumed, that is a proportionate increase in all inputs leads to a similar proportionate increase in output. The axes in Figure 3.1 can therefore represent input per unit of output, and the curve QQ' represents the unit isoquant, that is, those input combinations which yield one unit of output, assuming they are used efficiently.

The points A and B in the diagram represent the local education authorities whose levels of efficiency are being measured and compared. B lies on the isoquant and is therefore fully efficient, while A lies above B along a ray from the origin. A is therefore technically inefficient since it uses more of both inputs to produce the same output. The technical efficiency of A can be measured by the ratio OB/OA. A resulting ratio of 90 per cent, for example, would imply that A could produce the same level of output using 90 per cent of its inputs (and therefore at 90 per cent of its cost, assuming constant input prices). Technical inefficiency can therefore be measured as 1 - OB/OA and gives, in percentage terms, the cost saving that could be obtained by being 100 per cent efficient. An alternative, and very similar, measure of inefficiency would be the inverse of efficiency, OA/OB.

The isocost line in Figure 3.1, labelled CC', indicates the combinations of inputs x_1 and x_2 giving rise to the same level of expenditure. The slope of the isocost line is equal to the ratio of the two input prices, that is $(-)p_2/p_1$, where p_i denotes the price of x_i. The allocatively efficient input mix at any level of output will be the mix that minimizes the cost of producing the level of output in question, or, equivalently, the mix that

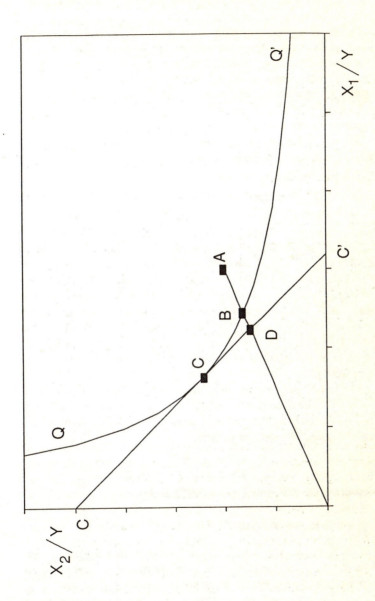

Figure 3.1: The Measurement of Efficiency

maximizes the level of output obtained from a fixed money outlay. In Figure 3.1 this occurs at point C. Here the slopes of the isocost line and the isoquant are the same.

Now it can be seen that authority B is also inefficient, since it is using the wrong input mix, given relative prices. This is allocative inefficiency. It is measured by 1 - OD/OB, and gives the proportionate increase in costs due to allocative inefficiency. A is similarly allocatively inefficient, in addition to its technical inefficiency. Its total efficiency may be measured by the ratio OD/OA, and its total inefficiency by 1 - OD/OA. This is approximately the sum of technical and allocative inefficiency.

We may formalise this still further by writing down the production and cost functions as follows:

(1) $Y = f(x)$ (production function)

(2) $C = c(p,Y)$ (cost function)

where Y measures output, x is a vector of inputs into the production process, C is total cost, and p is a vector of input prices. It is important to realise that the production function gives the maximum level of output possible, given the inputs, while the cost function gives the minimum cost of producing output Y given the costs of the various inputs. Thus these are frontier functions. It is quite possible (indeed likely) that actual output will be below the frontier, and that actual cost will be above its theoretical minimum. Inefficiency may thus be measured by the extent to which output falls short of the amount in equation (1) above, given the level of inputs, or by the extent to which costs exceed the level in equation (2), given input prices and the level of output.

The formal presentation given above focuses attention on several issues which are important in the field of efficiency measurement. Once these have been examined, different methods of measuring performance can be assessed by reference to them.

Measuring the Different Types of Inefficiency

Cost and Production Functions

One useful aspect of the formal approach is that inefficiency can be seen to be of two types. The remedy for each is different. Allocative inefficiency implies that inputs are being used efficiently, but that the wrong input mix is being used, and the remedy requires that input proportions be altered, for example altering the ratio of doctors to nursing staff in a hospital. Remedying technical inefficiency does not mean altering the input mix, but requires greater productivity from all inputs.

Measuring inefficiency means obtaining and working with information about either the production or cost function, but the results from each are different. Estimating a production function from actual data means that only technical inefficiency can be observed. The input proportions are treated as exogenous, and therefore no inefficiency is apportioned to the input mix. Estimating the cost function gives a measure of total inefficiency, because input proportions are assumed to be endogenous, in other words, at the discretion of the authority. However, the breakdown of efficiency into its technical and allocative components is not possible. The production function approach does not measure allocative efficiency because it does not make use of information on factor prices. To be able to measure allocative inefficiency one must make use of data on prices.

Objectives and Technology

The technical inefficiency of A can be measured with reference to B, which uses inputs in the same proportions. If authority B did not exist, A's inefficiency would have to be measured with reference to the unit isoquant at point B. This means that the production or cost function has to be estimated. A wide variety of functional forms are available for this purpose, or alternatively, no functional form at all need be imposed (see the discussion of Data Envelopment Analysis below). This is referred to as parametric versus non-parametric estimation. Advocates of the parametric approach argue that there must exist some underlying physical relationship between output and inputs, and that efficiency can only be measured relative to this. The non-parametric approach imposes no functional form, the argument being that imposing a particular form can be too restrictive and therefore result in poor estimation of levels of efficiency.

Statistical Noise

In practice, inefficiency is measured as a residual, rather than being estimated directly. This means that there is a danger of confusing inefficiency with statistical 'noise'. In regression analysis the residual is often called the 'error' term, and occurs because of a number of possible factors, such as measurement error or omitted variables. It is treated as a random variable and has a particular probability distribution. If part of the residual is now to be an inefficiency component, the problem becomes one of trying to disentangle it from the random part.

Models which take no account of statistical noise are termed deterministic, while those that do are called stochastic (the terms non-statistical and statistical are also used). It would seem important at least to consider the likely extent of statistical noise in the model, even if only informally. For example, a school may have an unusually large intake one year (more likely now with open enrolment) which affects its unit costs, or a local health authority may have to cope with an epidemic.

A more important point is that for non-statistical models one has no idea of the uncertainty surrounding the efficiency estimates, whereas for statistical models one has a range of test statistics such as standard errors, t-ratios, etc. which allow one to judge the quality of the model as it fits the data.

Finding the Frontier

Much of econometrics has been concerned with estimating production functions using regression techniques. It is only recently however that estimation methods have incorporated the fact that the production function is a frontier. The traditional regression approach places a line or plane through the data, which implies that some authorities are operating above the production frontier. The regression line thus gives the relationship between output and inputs for the average authority, not the frontier one.

The frontier which is being sought can be thought of either as the conceivable frontier or as the best practice frontier. The former measures what it is possible to achieve, though there might be no authority which is on the frontier; the latter measures the best that is achieved in practice by some authority (which may not be in the sample). In practice this distinction is not very important, as one can only make use of information that is in the sample, so that the best practice frontier is what is revealed. As the sample size increases, the distinction between these two concepts diminishes.

The Available Methodologies

Figure 3.2 below presents the different methodologies that have been applied to the measurement of efficiency, and places each in the appropriate category, according to whether the method is deterministic or stochastic, parametric or non-parametric.

I shall briefly discuss each of these methods in turn.

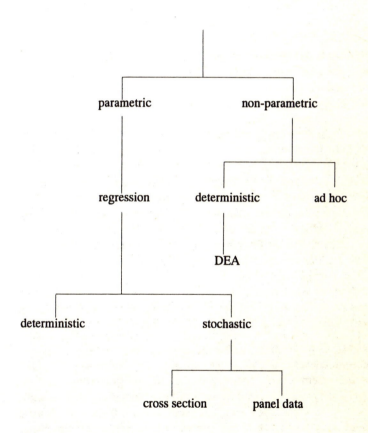

Figure 2: Different Methods of Efficiency Measurement

Ad Hoc Methods

These include such approaches as the use of pupil-teacher ratios in schools, or staffing ratios in local authority departments. Not much will be said about these methods except that it is a major problem to evaluate their results. Inefficiency could occur if the pupil-teacher ratio were either too high or too low. There has to be some idea of where the optimum lies before inefficiency can be inferred. These informal methods rarely take account of any technological relationships underlying the process of provision of services, nor of any statistical noise that may be present.

The Regression Model

This falls into the parametric category because some particular functional form has to be chosen to fit the data, for example the Cobb-Douglas formulation. Thus the regression model does suppose some form of technology to be estimated, relating output to inputs.

As mentioned earlier, the standard regression model fits an average curve to the data. The frontier may then be found by a number of different methods. If the model is a deterministic one, where the whole of the residual is assumed to measure inefficiency, then the regression line can be shifted upwards (in the case of a production function, down for a cost function), until all residuals are non-negative, and at least one zero. One may then equate these new residuals with inefficiency, so that the average level of inefficiency in the sample may be observed, as well as the level for each authority, and its ranking. It is implicitly assumed here that the slope coefficients of the frontier regression line are the same as for the ordinary regression line.

It seems more reasonable however to suppose a stochastic model, where the problem arises of trying to disentangle the statistical noise from inefficiency. The model may be written as follows:

(3) $Y_i = \beta_0 + \Sigma_j \beta_j x_{ij} + v_i + u_i$

where i indexes authorities, j the explanatory variables, and $v_i + u_i$ is a composed error term consisting of the random component v and the inefficiency term u.v would typically follow a Normal distribution, while u would be a one sided error term such that $u < 0$. The half Normal distribution is one that has been used in some studies.u therefore measures the extent to which each authority lies below the stochastic frontier,

$Y_i = \beta_0 + \Sigma_j \beta_j x_{ij} + v_i$.

Disentangling u from v + u can be done in different ways. If particular probability distributions are chosen for v and u, then maximum likelihood estimation procedures can be used. A simpler approach is to use 'corrected' ordinary least squares (COLS, see Richmond, 1974), which essentially searches for asymmetry in the composed error term for evidence about u. u itself is likely to have an asymmetric distribution, with most authorities lying quite close to the frontier, but a few lying much further away. Thus, for example, if the composed error turned out to be symmetric (that is, the third moment of the distribution equalled zero) then this would be evidence of no significant inefficiency existing. These procedures lead to a similar shift to the ordinary least squares regression line as in the deterministic case, except that the shift is smaller, since only part of the residual is due to inefficiency.

In the stochastic model it is not possible to measure the actual level of inefficiency for each authority because of the presence of the unobservable term v. The average level of u can be obtained (since on average $v = 0$), and further, one can obtain the expected value of u for each authority given the observed value of the composed error term for the authority. These expected values will give different estimates of the levels of efficiency for each authority than in the deterministic model, although the rankings of authorities will be the same.

The above methods make use of cross section data for authorities. If panel data (pooled time series and cross section) are available then an alternative presents itself. If v is a random error term, then it should average out to zero over time. The model may now be written as

(4) $Y_{it} = \beta_0 + \Sigma_j \beta_j x_{ijt} + v_{it} + u_i$

where t indexes time periods. There is assumed to be a common underlying data generation process for each time period in the data set.

Estimating this model allows observation of the composed error term for each authority for each time period. Averaging these error terms over time for each authority will reveal the value of u_i, the level of inefficiency for each authority. This is an advantage over the use of cross-section data alone. Some strong assumptions are made in the estimation of this model, in particular that the level of inefficiency is constant over time. If it is not, then the division of the composed error term into noise and inefficiency will not be accurate. Note however, that if levels of inefficiency are changing, then using cross-section data for only one year will yield a 'snapshot' of the position that may not be valid in other years.

Data Envelopment Analysis

DEA falls into the category of a non-parametric form of efficiency measurement, and does not use any particular functional form to relate outputs to inputs. It may best be explained with the aid of Figure 3.3, which is similar to Figure 3.1. Constant returns to scale are again assumed for simplicity of exposition.

Here there are five authorities (A to E), each producing a single output (Y) with 2 inputs (x_1 and x_2). In the absence of information on the exact location of the unit isoquant, one cannot suppose A, B, C or D to be technically inefficient. Authority B uses more of x_1 than authority A, but less of x_2. Further, authority B uses more x_2 than authority C, but less x_1. There are grounds, however, for believing authority E to be technically inefficient: it uses more of both inputs than authority C and yet produces no more output.

Measuring the technical efficiency of an authority requires an estimate of the location of the efficiency frontier. Farrell (1957) proceeded by assuming that the latter is never upward-sloping and is always convex to the origin. Convexity means that if two input bundles can each produce one unit of output, then so can any weighted average of them. DEA finds such an efficiency frontier by finding the line segments AB, BC, and CD which envelope the data. All observations then lie on or above the efficiency frontier. See Figure 3.3.

Measuring the efficiency of authorities is then done in a similar way to that depicted earlier. For an authority such as E in Figure 3.3, its efficiency is measured as OE*/OE, where OE* is at the intersection of the efficiency frontier and a ray from the origin to point E. This is a measure of technical efficiency. Because the ray from the origin passes through the line segment BC, E is being compared to a weighted average of authorities B and C. B and C are referred to as the 'peer group' of E, and each inefficient authority will have its own peer group. Where there are more than two inputs required to produce output, there will in general be more than two authorities in any peer group.

The efficiency frontier so constructed is not an isoquant, but a piece-wise-linear approximation to it. Thus the technology itself is not estimated. The approach is also deterministic rather than stochastic, so one should talk of 'measurement' rather than 'estimation', and no information about the reliability attached to this form of measurement is available. Thus on both questions of statistical noise and whether to use a parametric approach, DEA adopts a different approach from the regression model.

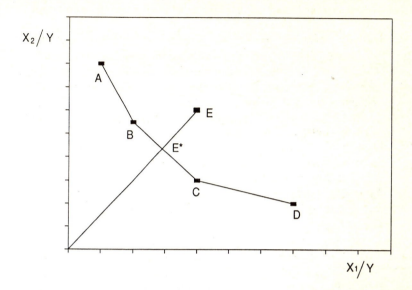

Figure 3.3: DEA:Single Output Case

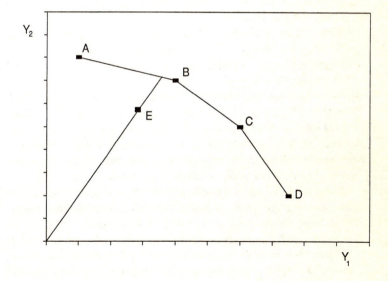

Figure 3.4: DEA: Multiple Output Case

One practical advantage of DEA is that it is straightforward to incorporate multiple outputs as well as inputs into the model. Figure 4 shows this case, where five authorities are producing different combinations of two outputs, Y_1 and Y_2, using (it is assumed) the same inputs. Authorities A, B, C and D form the efficiency frontier, while E is inefficient relative to the peer group A and B. Notice that A and D, producing the greatest amounts of Y_1 and Y_2 respectively, necessarily form part of the frontier, by virtue of being at the extremes of the line. This observation can be generalised to say that any authority with the largest ratio of any one output to any one input necessarily forms part of the efficiency frontier and is assessed to be 100 per cent efficient.

Presenting the problem of measuring the efficiency of an authority via the DEA technique in a formal manner brings out this point. The problem may be specified as follows, where there are m inputs and s outputs, and the efficiency of the authority indexed 0 is being measured:

$$(5) \quad \max_{w_r, z_i} h_0 = \frac{\Sigma_r w_r Y_{ro}}{\Sigma_i z_i X_{io}}$$

subject to

$$\frac{\Sigma_r w_r Y_{rj}}{\Sigma_i z_i X_{ij}} < 1 \qquad j = 0...n$$

$$w_r, z_i > 0 \qquad i = 1...m, r = 1...s$$

Here, Y_{rj}, $X_{ij} > 0$ represent outputs and inputs of the jth authority, and the w_r, z_i are weights to be assigned to the outputs and inputs respectively. The maximand h_0 is the efficiency ratio for authority 0, the ratio of its weighted outputs to weighted inputs. The problem is to find weights w and z to maximise the efficiency ratio of the authority, subject to no authority having an efficiency ratio exceeding unity using these weights. The solution method ensures that $0 < \max h_0 < 1$, with a fully efficient authority having a score of one. If an authority is inefficient, this means that there exists no set of weights w_r, z_i such that its efficiency ratio exceeds or equals that of every other authority in the sample.

Suppose that authority 0 has the highest ratio of output 1 to input 3 of any authority in the sample. Then by choosing w_1 to be arbitrarily large, and all other (input and output) weights to be arbitrarily small, we can guarantee to make authority 0 appear 100 per cent efficient. In practical terms, this means that 'unusual' authorities, or outliers, will always appear to be 100 per cent efficient, which may not be desirable. The authority might be extremely inefficient at producing all other outputs, for example. Note that a parametric approach will not have this characteristic, since outliers need not necessarily fall on the efficiency frontier.

Further insight into the DEA technique may be gained by further consideration of the weights. Their obvious interpretation, to the economist at least, is as prices of the outputs and inputs. Then (5) simply represents the ratio of revenues to costs. However, DEA does not simply use market prices as the weights, but searches for any set of relative prices at which the authority will appear efficient. If there is some set of prices at which the authority has the highest revenue/cost ratio, then it is deemed 100 per cent efficient. Furthermore, as more outputs and inputs are included in the model, more authorities become 100 per cent efficient, due to their being the extreme authority in some dimension.

DEA therefore tends to show authorities in a favourable light, since it searches for the best possible weights for an authority. The results may therefore set an upper bound to the efficiency of authorities. This property of showing authorities in the most favourable light is seen as a virtue of DEA by some commentators, since it allows authorities to choose their own objectives (that is, outputs) rather than be constrained to follow centrally determined goals. This might be particularly important in the case of local government for example, which is supposed to be autonomous of central government in the way in which it carries out its tasks. Each authority is only compared on efficiency grounds with a (typically small) subset of other authorities which roughly shares those objectives - its peer group.

Where appropriate markets exist, the weights emerging from DEA could be compared with prices, to get some idea of allocative efficiency, rather than just technical efficiency. This seems to be done rarely in practice, but is an interesting avenue for further research.

Critics of DEA (see Schmidt 1985-6, for example) regard this flexibility as excessive. Although the objectives of authorities may differ, the underlying production function relating outputs to inputs ought to be the same, and this should be estimated before any assertions about efficiency are made. Therefore, outlying authorities should still be judged on the basis of the same technological relationships that affect all authorities, and not be deemed efficient just because they are different in their choice of outputs. Estimation of a common underlying production relationship is therefore likely to reduce the number of authorities which are judged efficient.

Applying the Models to Education

The above analysis is now applied to the field of education, where a number of different studies have been carried out, using the different techniques. The analyses have used similar but not identical data, so comparison of results has to be somewhat informal. Briefly, the studies and the methods they used are as follows:

(a) The Department of Education and Science (DES, 1983; DES, 1984) used regression techniques to look at examination performance. Theirs is therefore a parametric analysis, using a straightforward linear regression model. They estimated a production function type model, the output being various measures of exam performance, the explanatory variables being inputs such as expenditure on teachers and also a number of socio-economic background variables. Statistical noise is dealt with informally by averaging the exam performance measures for each authority over a number of years. The frontier is also found by informal methods: authorities are judged to be efficient or not if they lie more than two standard deviations from the regression line. No overall measure of efficiency is given, nor are standard errors of the coefficients.

(b) Jesson, Mayston and Smith (1987) used DEA to measure LEA performance taking two measures of exam performance as outputs, and total expenditure per pupil and three socio-economic background variables as inputs. As in the DES studies only technical efficiency is measured. The model is a deterministic, non-parametric one, so that there is no way of measuring the reliability of the results obtained. Efficiency measures and rankings for all LEAs are obtained, as well as an overall measure of efficiency for the sample.

(c) I have used the same data set to estimate a frontier cost function using both cross-section and panel data for the five years 1980/81 to 1984/85 (Barrow, 1991). The number of authorities in the sample was restricted because of the need for a run of data over five years for the panel model, and only 57 (out of 96) authorities provided a consistent set. The explanatory variables in the cost function were one measure of output (percentage of pupils with five graded passes at O-level), and several measures of socio-economic background, such as the additional educational needs variable used in rate support grant calculations. Statistical noise and the problem of finding the frontier were dealt with in the manner set out above, in the section on the regression model.

Comparison of Results

The simplest way of comparing results across different studies is to look at rankings, particularly at the extremes of the distributions where attention is likely to be focused.

Table 3.1 below compares results from my own work with those of Jesson, Mayston and Smith (1987) (the data for this were kindly provided by Peter Smith). The authorities chosen are from both extremes of the efficiency distribution according to the panel data method of estimation.

Table 3.1: Comparison of Results

Authority	*J,M & S* Efficiency (%)	rank[1]	*Barrow* Panel data Efficiency (%)	rank[2]	Cross section[4] Efficiency (%)	rank[2]
Essex	90	92	72	57	89	51
Kent	97	53	72	56	91	43
Hants	97	47	78	55	95	21
Sheffield	97	52	79	54	86	57
Lancs	90	93	81	53	95	19
Cheshire	92	90	82	52	93	36
Norfolk	88	95	90	28	92	42
Cornwall	99	39[3]	100	1	94	25
Wolverhampton	100	1=	98	2	98	3
Shropshire	93	81	97	3	94	31
East Sussex	100	1=	96	4	94	26

Notes
1. Out of 96.
2. Out of 57.
3. Note that since 32 authorities were 100 per cent efficient, this ranking is quite high.
4. Deterministic frontier model.

It can be seen that there is a reasonable degree of agreement among the methods, but with a few spectacular differences. Hampshire appears to be reasonably efficient according to the DEA method, but near the bottom using panel data (from a simple cross-section regression, Hampshire appears to be just above half-way). From the DEA results it appears that Hampshire's efficiency is heavily influenced by the proportion of pupils obtaining three or more graded passes, which may be interpreted as success with lower ability children. This variable is not included in the panel data model, so this may explain the discrepancy which arises.

Shropshire is near the top by the panel data method but near the bottom according to DEA. Unfortunately, the DEA results do not suggest why Shropshire should be inefficient, except that the proportion of children from one parent families is a 'slack' variable, meaning that an increase in this would not affect the authority's measured efficiency. This variable constitutes part of the additional educational needs variable included in the regression model, so this should not explain the difference in rankings.

The cross-section and panel data models also give quite different rankings on occasion, although they use the same data sample. This may be evidence of significant year to year fluctuations in the data, and it indicates that one should perhaps be wary of drawing conclusions from one year's data alone. The rank correlation coefficient between the different years' rankings ranges between 1 and 0.61, getting smaller as the years being compared lie further apart.

The average level of inefficiency also varies according to the method of measurement as shown in Table 3.2.

Table 3.2: Comparative Levels of Inefficiency

DEA	3.2%
Cross section model	
deterministic	11%-20% (depending upon year)
stochastic	4%-7%
Panel data model	16%

It can be seen that the average level of inefficiency depends very much upon the method of measurement. The cross-section model is interesting in that it suggests that noise predominates over inefficiency, and an average level of inefficiency of between four per cent and seven per cent would not seem to be excessive. DEA measures inefficiency at only 3.2 per cent (using a deterministic model), but this is only technical efficiency and ignores the allocative component. It should be recalled that DEA tends to give an optimistic view of each authority's performance.

The panel data result is somewhat curious since it gives a much higher estimate of total inefficiency than the cross-section case. If efficiency were varying over time (either its average level or the distribution amongst authorities), then fitting a panel data model to the whole sample might result in a poorer fit than fitting a cross-section model to each year individually. Indeed, if cross-section regressions are fitted for each year (not reported here), the individual regression coefficients can vary by as much as 50 per cent between their minimum and maximum values over the five years.

The DES results can be compared with those obtained using DEA. Unfortunately, the DES study only names authorities at the extremes of the distribution and few of these fall into my own sample. Of the eight efficient authorities in the DES study, six achieve a 100 per cent efficiency score by DEA. The other two achieve 97 per cent and 95 per cent, and are ranked 48th and 66th respectively. Of the five inefficient authorities, DEA gives low efficiencies for three, another achieves 97 per cent (ranked 51), while the final authority (Knowsley) scores a perfect 100 per cent! Knowsley does not appear to be particularly 'unbalanced' in comparison with other authorities achieving 100 per cent efficiency. In other words, its measured efficiency via DEA is not attributable to doing well on one particular output level or input usage (see Jesson, Mayston and Smith (1987), pp. 258-9 for further explanation).

Lessons for Efficiency Measurement

The most important point to be made is that efficiency can vary significantly according to the method of measurement used. Part of this difference may be put down to the type of inefficiency (technical or allocative) that is being measured, but even after accounting for this, substantial disagreements remain.

It is likely that at the heart of the problem lies the measurement of inefficiency as a residual, once everything else has been accounted for. Different methods of measuring what does influence costs or examination results can lead to large differences in the residual term. This is similar to the problem of estimating the balance of payments. Small errors in the estimation of either imports or exports can lead to a huge error in the estimate of the trade balance.

It is clear that care needs to be taken in the interpretation of the results of efficiency studies. The problems of measurement noted here appear at quite a high level of aggregation, and the problems might become even greater if one were to try to compare the performance of individual schools, for example. At this more disaggregated level the problems of statistical noise would probably be more prevalent.

These types of study should therefore be used with circumspection, and may be used as pointers to the need for more detailed studies at the micro level of analysis in some authorities.

Although the studies and methods outlined here may appear to be fairly abstract and statistically complex, they do throw some useful light upon the measurement of efficiency and can be an aid to the interpretation of even more informal studies. Consideration of the nature of inefficiency itself, of the possible existence of statistical noise in the data, and of whether there is some underlying physical relationship between outputs and inputs in the area under scrutiny, is a useful part of any investigation.

References

Barrow, M., (1991), Measuring the Performance of Local Education Authorities:A Frontier Approach, *Economics of Education Review* 10(1), forthcoming.

Barrow, M., and Wagstaff,A., (1989), 'Efficiency Measurement in the Public Sector: An Appraisal', *Fiscal Studies*, 10, 72-97.

Charnes, A., Cooper, W. W. and Rhodes, E., (1978), 'Measuring the Efficiency of Decision-Making Units, *European Journal of Operational Research*, 2, 429-444.

Charnes, A., Cooper, W. W. and Rhodes, E., (1981), 'Evaluating Program and Managerial Efficiency: An Application of Data Envelopment Analysis to Program Follow Through', *Management Science* 27, 668-697.

Department of Education and Science, (1983), *School Standards and Spending: A Statistical Analysis*, Statistical Bulletin 16/83, HMSO, London.

Department of Education and Science, (1984), *School Standards and Spending: A Further Appreciation*, Statistical Bulletin 13/84, HMSO, London.

Farrell, M. J., (1957), 'The Measurement of Productive Efficiency', *Journal of the Royal Statistical Society*, Series A 120: 253-266.

Jesson, D., Mayston, D., and Smith, P., (1987), 'Performance Assessment in the Education Sector: Educational and Economic Perspectives', *Oxford Review of Education*, 13: 249-266.

Schmidt, P., (1986), 'Frontier Production Functions', *Econometric Reviews*,4, 289-328.

Schmidt, P. and Sickles, R. C., (1984), 'Production Frontiers and Panel Data', *Journal of Business and Economic Statistics*,2, 367-374.

Chapter 4

The Use of Output and Performance Measures in Government Departments

Sue Lewis and Jeff Jones*

Introduction

This chapter discusses how output and performance measures (OPMs) are used in government departments, some of the barriers to their use and how these are being overcome. The chapter begins with a short section describing the main management initiatives which have contributed to the development of OPMs, the role of the Treasury in implementing the initiatives, and a brief summary of the terminology used. The second section describes the use of OPMs while the third outlines some problems which have to be overcome.

Background

The use of OPMs in government departments goes back at least twenty years. The Land Registry, for example, has published productivity indices for the whole department since 1968-69 and collected productivity and quality of service indicators for local area offices since 1972. Other early users of OPMs include the Department of Employment and the Inland Revenue.

These early measures had several common features: they described the performance of executive functions, the relevant outputs were easily identifiable and measurable and the inputs (cost and staff time) could be aligned with the outputs. They were also concerned with measuring the implementation of policies rather than the effects.

---

*   The views expressed here are of the authors and not of their Department.

The Financial Management Initiative (FMI), launched in 1982 (HMT, 1983, 1984, 1987, FMI, 1986), was the first initiative specifically to encourage the development of OPMs (although the notion of accountable management dates back to the Fulton Report of 1968). The Multi-departmental Review of Budgeting (HMT, 1986a, 1986b, 1988a) reinforced this message. The main philosophy underlying both initiatives was that managers at all levels should be responsible and accountable for their sphere of operations. This necessitated detailed budgets, held at an appropriate level of delegation, and supporting OPMs.

Departments continued developing OPMs throughout the mid-1980s. A number of case studies showing their progress can be found in two Treasury Working Papers (Output, 1986 and 1987). Although these cover both running (ie administrative) costs and programme expenditure, it is fair to say the emphasis was on measuring the outputs associated with running costs. This was mainly because this was technically an easier task.

A further initiative on policy evaluation (1985), attempted to redress the balance (HMT, 1988). Although not all policies are programme-related, the initiative helped focus departments' attention on programme areas. It is now government policy that all new policy proposals should be accompanied by an evaluation plan, and that all existing policies should be reviewed periodically. To do this, departments need to be able to define clear objectives, monitor progress against them, and evaluate the outcomes.

The push for better management in departments received further impetus from the Running Costs initiative. Since 1987 departments have been required to produce for each Survey a Management Plan, covering all their running costs expenditure for the three forward years and including commitments to cumulative efficiency gains of at least 1.5 per cent of their total running costs provision.

Finally, OPMs are essential for 'Next Steps' Executive Agencies (Efficiency Unit, 1988; HMT, 1989c). Many will want to introduce performance-related pay which will require robust and appropriate measures of performance. All will be required to publish key performance targets.

Role of the Treasury

With the exception of 'Next Steps', the initiatives described above were all Treasury-led. The Treasury also plays a significant role in setting up Executive Agencies. The focus for all this work is Treasury expenditure divisions, which monitor the implementation of the various initiatives in 'their' departments.

There is also a substantial input from Treasury specialists, who advise expenditure divisions and departments on the technical aspects. For OPMs Treasury guidance to departments takes a number of forms, for example:

- issuing written guidance and examples of good practice (most recently a guide on OPMs for Executive Agencies);
- working with departments to improve specific areas;
- participating in courses and seminars at the Civil Service College and in departments.

There are no easy measures of the Treasury's success in persuading departments to develop and use OPMs. Of published documents, the Public Expenditure White Paper (HMT, 1989a), probably offers the best indication. Figures for the number of OPMs for 1986 and 1989 are shown in Table 4.1, which also shows how they are broken down by the types defined below.

Table 4.1: Numbers of OPMs

Type of indicator		*1986*	*1989*
Economy		32	150
Efficiency		132	265
Effectiveness		222	556
Quality of service		63	110
Other (mainly output measures)		771	1246
	Total	1220	2327

By itself, a simple count is not a good indicator of the value of the information. To present a coherent picture, OPMs should be compared with targets or plans, or with previous years.

From this point of view, the value of the information increased greatly: the number of comparisons of outturn with earlier targets or plans went from 52 in 1986 to 549 in 1989. The number of measures presented as time series (rather than single figures) also increased considerably. The Treasury no longer publishes a count of the OPMs in the PEWP, because the number is now felt to be about right. In any case, the PEWP will be replaced by departmental reports in 1991; transition arrangements are already in place. The only other quantitative evidence of the Treasury's success is the number of departments judged to have satisfactory arrangements on performance measurement as part of the Multi-departmental

Review of Budgeting (MDRB). An internal Treasury review of progress on MDRB, conducted in April 1989, showed that 26 out of 34 departments met this requirement. Action plans for improvement have been agreed with the other eight; these are currently being implemented.

Terminology

Despite the wealth of literature on OPMs in both the public and private sectors, there do not appear to be universal definitions of the '3Es' (economy, efficiency and effectiveness). The descriptions below are those recommended by the Treasury, and used by most government departments.

Economy - the extent to which the cost of inputs is minimised. In practice, this is usually measured in terms of money saved by switching to cheaper inputs. For example, reductions secured through market testing, or through using lower quality inputs (for example second rather than first class post).

Efficiency - the relationship of the output of an activity or organisation to the associated inputs. The most commonly used measures of efficiency are labour productivity and unit cost.

Effectiveness - the extent to which output contributes to final objectives. This is often very difficult to measure, although it can be inferred in broad terms from intermediate indicators.

The term 'value for money' is frequently used in government departments. It literally means the final social and economic benefit of an activity in relation to the cost. However, in common usage, it has become a shortened description for the '3Es'; cutting costs at the expense of efficiency, for example, would not count as value for money.

Other terms are defined as they appear in this chapter. A glossary can be found in several government publications, including *Policy Evaluation: A Guide for Managers* (HMT, 1988b).

What is Measured

There is a great diversity of activities in central government. Figure 4.1 shows a rough typology of activities with examples. Figure 4.2 shows the main characteristics of OPMs for each type, with illustrations.

Performance measurement is easiest for organisations which carry out a single type of activity, particularly where this is volume processing or

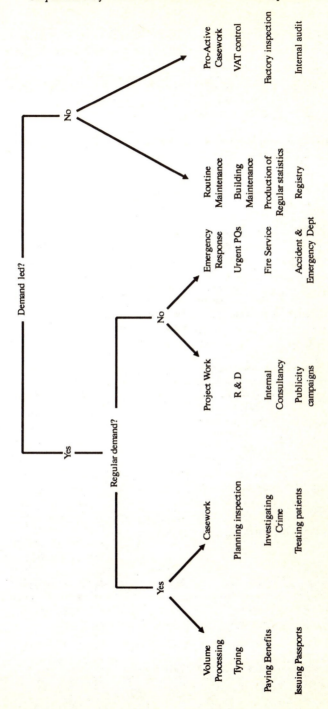

Figure 4.1: A Typology of Activities

Type of activity	Characteristics	Outputs	Performance Indicators
Volume processing	Standard (i.e. little variation between items) Often rule-based	Numbers of items dealt with	Quality (e.g. error rates, timeliness) Staff productivity Unit cost
Casework	Variation between cases may be great Often an element of professional judgement	Number of cases completed (weighted if necessary to allow for complexity)	As above but quality assessment may involve peer review and/or customer satisfaction
Project work	Individual items of work. Often a cost-benefit analysis is needed at the outset Outcomes may be uncertain	May have deliverable milestones - e.g. reports, prototypes Numbers of projects completed may be meaningful for some research programmes	Variance from cost and time profiles. Measures of technical success. Quality (often judged by peer review)
Emergency response	Demand may be unpredictable and sporadic but cases need to be dealt with immediately they arise. Implies excess capacity needs to be built in to cover peak demands	Capacity - Numbers of incidents dealt with	Speed of response Effectiveness (lives or value of property saved)
Routine maintenance	Standard routine activities	Volume of work done	Variance from plan. Productivity/Unit costs/ Accuracy (or other quality measures)
Pro-active casework	Often preventative or regulatory activities.	As for casework	As for casework, plus success rates (e.g. amount of underdeclared tax discovered)

Figure 4.2: Main Characteristics of OPMs

casework. Hence at one end of the scale there are the large 'paper factories' such as the Department of Social Security and DVLC, where performance measurement is well integrated into management decision making. At the other end there are complex organisations such as police forces, which carry out activities of virtually every variety.

Uses of OPMs

OPMs can be used as analytical tools to support a range of management decisions in the following:
- planning;
- monitoring and control;
- reporting;
- evaluation.

This section describes briefly how OPMs can be used in the planning cycle and then considers in more detail the topical areas of management plans, policy evaluation and Executive Agencies. What follows is a general picture demonstrating that practice varies from department to department.

The Planning Cycle

In planning, OPMs are mainly used to help set targets and allocate resources. Typically, historical values of performance indicators are used together with a model relating inputs, outputs and performance. This may involve components such as Ministerial targets for quality of service, productivity targets based on changes in working practices, and forecasts of demand. Data on demand and productivity can be used to deduce the level of resources needed to achieve the quality of service targets.

The process operates in a similar way for pro-active activities.In the case of building inspection, for example, resource levels might be based on visiting all 'high-risk' premises once a month and others once a year, given targets for visits per person. When departments have completed their internal planning arrangements they submit to the Treasury the following:
- a management plan, which is required to demonstrate efficiency improvements of at least one and a half per cent a year for running costs expenditure;

- a 'value for money' statement for their programme expenditure,
  which shows what the baseline (ie previously agreed
  expenditure) will buy. This should cover outputs, efficiency and
  quality of service measures.

The above cover the three years of the Public Expenditure Survey, and
help the Treasury to assess bids for extra resources.

OPMs are used in-year to monitor against plans. Divergences can be
used to forecast the likely end of year levels of output, expenditure or
service quality, and to indicate appropriate control action. This may
involve in-year corrective action, for example redeployment of staff or
changing the timing of a major purchase.

Finally, OPMs are used to report on achievement, both up the management chain and publicly. Many departments publish annual reports
with performance indicators: examples of titles can be found in the
bibliographies of departmental PEWP chapters (HMT, 1989a).

Management Plans

Since the abolition of the manpower ceilings at the end of 1987-88,
control of departments' use of administrative resources has been exercised principally through the system of cash provision for running costs
introduced in 1986-87. Since the 1987 Public Expenditure Survey departments have been required to prepare three-year management plans which
demonstrate how they will deliver measurable cumulative efficiency
gains of at least one and a half per cent a year. Where appropriate, and in
particular in large executive operations, much higher annual targets are
expected.

All running costs gains attributable to management action (rather than
outside circumstances) may contribute towards these efficiency targets.
This may include higher quality or levels of output for an agreed priority
service, or cash savings through the use of reduced resources for the same
levels of output. Economy savings may also be allowable, particularly
where outputs cannot be measured. 'Windfall' gains, accruing, for
example, from reduced demand, do not count.

Some departments found it helpful to construct a 'total factor' productivity index for all their running costs expenditure (for example, Environment) but this is not always easy (see Chapter 9 below). Where significant
proportions of running costs expenditure are incurred in headquarters
policy divisions this approach can cause problems. Although some as-

pects of policy work are measurable, for example dealing with parliamentary questions, much of it is not.

Departments faced with large proportions of unmeasurable activities tend, therefore, to identify savings from specific management actions, such as:

- relocating;
- contracting out of services (for example through market testing);
- improving purchasing (e.g. through market testing) or stockholding.

Policy Evaluation

In parallel with the regular planning and monitoring activities described earlier, departments have a rolling programme for evaluating their policies. All Cabinet Papers containing new proposals with value for money implications should state the following:

- what is to be achieved;
- by when;
- at what cost;
- how achievement is to be measured.

Policies announced during or after the 1987 General Election are subject to this instruction. Departments also periodically evaluate policies which have been in existence for some time, to check whether the objectives are still valid and whether they are being met in the most cost-effective way.

Figure 4.3 shows a typical evaluation framework, applicable to both new and existing policies. Drawing up an evaluation plan usually involves defining:

(a) Objectives. If a policy has been properly appraised, objectives should already be clearly defined and prioritised. Often this is not the case, and it is necessary to clarify existing statements on both final and intermediate objectives. The ultimate objective of the Home Office 'Magpie' campaign was to reduce crime, particularly domestic burglary. Intermediate objectives were to make the public aware of the risk and to persuade them to improve the physical security of their homes in particular, for example by purchasing, fitting and using window locks.

(b) A base case. This is a baseline with which to compare the impact of the policy. It could be the existing situation, although this is likely to involve some sophisticated 'what-if' modelling to project current

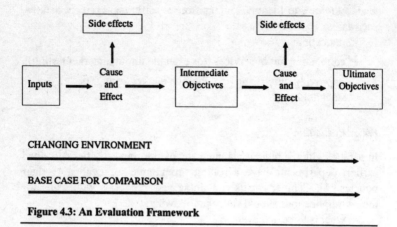

Figure 4.3: An Evaluation Framework

trends. A control group is ideal: this allows comparison between a situation where a policy is being implemented and one where it is not.

(c) Assumptions. The links between final and intermediate objectives rest on the assumption that there is a causal relationship between the two. These cause and effect assumptions are made explicit where possible. In the 'Magpies' example, one such assumption is that the fitting of security devices and operation of Neighbourhood Watch would have an observable effect on reported crime. It is also important to state assumptions relating to the external environment, for example about socio-economic factors.

Once an evaluation plan has been constructed, the task of collecting relevant information begins. Some examples of indicators which could have a bearing on the 'Magpies' evaluation are shown below. These are related to the framework diagram in Figure 4.3.

- *Inputs:* Amount of campaign advertising (measured by, for example, television rating points - TVRs).

- *Intermediate objectives:* Proportion of population who are aware of the campaign and changes in attitudes of target audience(s).

- *Final objectives:* Decrease in reported burglary and/or increase of proportion of failed burglaries.

At the time of writing there are few concrete examples of the results of evaluations feeding back into policy decisions. This is mainly due to the long lead time between drawing up an evaluation plan and getting meaningful results. But the next example shows how an evaluation of the Community Programme (which lasted from 1982 to 1988) relates to the development of Employment Training.

The Department of Employment evaluated the Community Programme (CP) through a series of surveys of CP participants and sponsors. The results showed, among other things, that some of the target group were under-represented in the scheme. Unemployed people with families to support (generally over the over-25s) could lose out financially by participating in CP, because their pay was lower than the benefit they would have otherwise received.

CP was set up as a work experience programme. However, a training element was introduced for some participants as the programme developed. Evidence from a small study suggested that those who received training had higher job placement rates. This factor supported the case for a new scheme with a greater training content.

A new programme for the unemployed, Employment Training, was introduced in 1988. It offers directed training as well as practical training on a project or at a work place. Participants who are generally involved full-time are paid an addition to their benefits. Early evaluation results suggest success in attracting a greater proportion of 'over-25s' in the target groups and job placement rates are higher than on CP.

Executive Agencies

In February 1988 the Efficiency Unit's report, 'Improving Management in Government: the Next Steps' was published (Efficiency Unit, 1988). The government accepted that, so far as practicable, the government's business should be run by Executive Agencies. These operate within agreed policy and resources frameworks. The framework document for each agency sets out the Chief Executive's responsibilities, delegated authorities and how performance is to be monitored. Within the framework, the Chief Executive is responsible and accountable for delivering results. One of the main aims of the initiative is to improve efficiency and quality of service to the customer. Ten agencies were launched in the period up to December 1989, by which time another 42 candidates had been announced (HMT, 1989c).

Output and performance measurement is, in principle, the same for Executive Agencies as for departments. However, there are important changes in emphasis, for example:

- departments (and the Treasury) will need to substitute strategic management for detailed day-to-day control. Thus their main focus will be on a few key areas of performance, measured at an aggregate level;
- Chief Executives' pay (and in some cases that of staff) may be related to the performance of the Agency as a whole;
- many Agencies will be financed mainly or wholly from receipts and be subject to an 'arms-length' financial regime; this may involve, for example, exemption from gross running costs control.

These considerations imply the need for robust measures of performance, both for Agency management and parent departments. It should be noted that while success in the market (where Agencies are trading) is a sufficient measure of performance, more detailed management information is needed for planning and accounting for stewardship of resources. Agencies are public bodies which remain publicly accountable for the management of their resources.

In many cases, Agencies' activities fall into the 'volume processing' or 'casework' categories, and measurement presents few problems. However, there are a number of research and development (R&D) establishments which exist as Agencies, or are Agency candidates. Typical indicators which are emerging for R&D establishments fall into three groups. Examples are shown below.

(a) Financial performance

- Income, split between parent department, other government departments and non-Exchequer bodies
- Non-Exchequer revenue as a per centage of total revenue.

(b) Quality of service

- Index of customer satisfaction (derived from the results of periodic surveys)
- Appointments and other distinctions earned by personnel
- Timeliness of output against agreed project milestones
- Proportion of quotations which are successful

(c) Administration

- Running costs per technical staff year
- Utilisation rate of chargeable staff
- Daily rate for senior scientific officer (based on full cost recovery)
- Overhead rate
- Ratio of support to technical staff numbers.

The group of indicators under (c) does not relate in a straightforward way to efficiency. However, they would normally be components of a management efficiency plan.

The measures given above are mostly directed towards measuring the performance of R&D administration. Effectiveness is of at least equal importance. As research establishments become Agencies, they will move towards a clearer customer-contractor relationship. Departments will therefore be responsible for assessing and evaluating their R&D programmes in the context of wider departmental objectives. They will then seek the contractor who can deliver the research most efficiently at a sufficiently high level of quality.

Overcoming Problems

Although departments have made great progress in developing and using OPMs, a number of problems remain. Some of these, and the emerging solutions, are discussed in this section.

Setting Measurable Objectives

This is an area which some departments find difficult. For example, objectives are frequently descriptions of what an organisation does, for example 'to liaise with ...', 'to report on ...', 'to arrange training courses ...'.

Where objectives are stated in this way, departments are encouraged to think about why the particular activity is performed. Often the ultimate answer is that it is a statutory requirement, or demand-led, in which case the activity can be thought of as a constraint rather than an objective. Objectives then need to be defined in terms of quality of service, for example: 'to process all applications within five working days' or 'to achieve a client satisfaction rating of at least 90 per cent'.

Another common shortcoming is a failure to quantify objectives. This is not always a serious problem. For example, objectives which start 'to improve' or 'to reduce' may be legitimate, provided the change is observable and its magnitude does not matter. Quantification can even be meaningless: 'to complete ten reports by April 1990' is only a useful objective if it is clear how it relates to some more ultimate objective. In general, departments are encouraged to quantify where it is meaningful.

Genuine difficulties arise where outputs are difficult to define (for example advisory activities); where control is limited (e.g. where an organisation operates through persuasion or negotiation); and where objectives conflict. The last case is quite common and can sometimes be resolved through quantifying the trade-offs between competing objectives. For example, safety regulations designed to reduce accidents may increase compliance costs. There are well-established methods for costing deaths and injury from accidents, so in principle the link between costs and benefits can be calculated.

Measurement and Aggregation

Most of the remaining measurement problems are technical. How can the quantity and quality of advice be measured? How should the use of assets be accounted for in unit costs? Work continues in these areas, particularly in the context of setting up Executive Agencies.

One of the barriers to constructing measures of unit cost is a general lack of cost information, particularly on capital. This situation is being rapidly remedied. A Treasury working group is currently looking at the way departments account for the use of capital assets, with a view to encouraging the setting up of asset registers, the inclusion of capital charges in management accounts and development of measures of asset use.

Another area of current interest is the measurement of quality of service. Attention is focussed on this both in the context of Next Steps agencies, and as a result of concern expressed by the Public Accounts Committee (PAC, 1987/8, 1989b). This arose from an examination of the quality of service to the public at local social security offices.

The Treasury, in its response to the PAC, promised to 'issue guidance to departments on the use of surveys and other methods for assessing the quality of services they provide to the public'. This is underway.

Finally, considerable work is going into devising aggregate measures of performance. It is not usually sensible to aggregate different types of measure (for example efficiency and quality) although in principle this can be done for a particular activity. Some measures are simply impossible to add together, for example crimes which are cleared-up and crimes which are prevented.

Most effort has been directed at developing aggregate measures of efficiency, particularly for Executive Agencies. Generally, the approach is to construct an index of efficiency changes, relative to a base year. Outputs are weighted by base year unit costs, to allow a common unit of measurement. Inputs can either be measured by volume (in the same way as outputs), or by cost.

In the first case, this gives an index of physical productivity. This has several drawbacks:

- it is sensitive to the mix of outputs. This means the weights need to be updated periodically.

- it is price-independent, so neither wasteful management (for example a doubling of pay rates) or efficient management (for example capital-labour substitution), will show up.

This implies that an aggregate productivity measure of this type should only be used at a management level where there is little or no control over the mix and price of input resources.

In the second case where inputs are measured in cost terms, it can be argued that the resulting efficiency index is a better measure of managerial performance, where management has the freedom to react to relative price changes by substituting one input for another. But several questions remain in relation to this index. For example, how should it be adjusted for price changes? And how should asset values be included? For example, if assets are revalued, measured efficiency will deteriorate.

Integrating OPMs into the Management Process

Departments vary considerably in the extent to which OPMs are integrated into the decision-making process and, subsequently, the Public Expenditure Survey. There is evidence of the following problems:

- information for the Treasury (Management Plans/value for money statements) is often collected as a separate exercise. Consequently, it is regarded as a bureaucratic burden rather than an integral part of management;

- information collected at divisional level is not analysed centrally and presented in such a way that it can be readily assimilated by top management and used to help decide priorities;

- some departments adopt a 'bottom-up' approach to OPMs. This means that line managers have insufficient direction on how to construct and present OPMs in a way that ensures consistency with departmental aims and objectives;
- insufficient attention is given to ensuring that action is taken as a result of annual performance reviews.

Use of Specialist Resources

Many of the problems discussed in this section could be overcome given sufficient resources. Developing OPMs and integrating them into departmental management can involve:

- investment and expertise in information technology;
- specialist help (OR people and accountants);
- investment in training managers to interpret and use OPMs.

As well as these 'set-up' costs, there has to be substantial and continuous input from line managers, finance divisions, etc. As departments move up the learning curve, and procedures become more automated, this overhead will reduce.

Conclusion

This chapter has only skated the surface of a complex and difficult subject. It is hoped that the reader will be left with the impression that departments have done much to improve their management of resources through the measurement of output and performance, and that inroads are being made into the remaining areas.

In the short term, most effort will be concentrated on ensuring that Executive Agencies can deliver measured improvements in efficiency and quality of service, and that their performance-related pay schemes are soundly based. This work, particularly where it involves the solution of technical problems, is likely to produce substantial benefits for departments.

References

Committee of Public Accounts, (1988), *Quality of Service to the Public at Local Social Security Offices,* Forty-fourth report, 1987-88, HMSO, London.

Efficiency Unit, (1988), *Improving Management in Government: the Next Steps. Report to the Prime Minister,* HMSO, London.

Financial Management in Government, (1983), Cm 9058, HMSO, London

HM Treasury, (1986a), *Multi-Departmental Review of Budgeting: Executive Summary,* London.

HM Treasury, (1986b), *Multi-Departmental Review of Budgeting: Final Central Report,* London.

HM Treasury, (1987), *Treasury Minute on the Eleventh to Sixteenth, Eighteenth and Nineteenth Reports from the Public Accounts Committee,* Cm 236, HMSO, London.

HM Treasury, (1988a), *Second Report on the Implementation of the Recommendations of the MDR of Budgeting,* Volume I, London.

HM Treasury, (1988b), *Policy Evaluation: A Guide for Managers,* London.

HM Treasury, (1989a), *The Government's Expenditure Plans* (PEWP) (1989-90 to 1991-92), January, Departmental volumes Cm 601 to Cm 619.

HM Treasury (1989b), *Treasury Minute on the 43rd to 48th Reports from the Committee of Public Accounts 1987-88,* Cm 563, HMSO, London.

HM Treasury, (1989c), *The Financing and Accountability of Next Steps Agencies,* Cm 914, London.

Output and Performance Measurement in Central Government: Progress in Departments, (1986), Treasury Working Paper No.38.

Output and Performance Measurement in Central Government: Some Practical Achievements, (1987), Treasury Working Paper No.45, London.

Progress in Financial Management in Government Departments, (1984), Cm 9297, HMSO, London.

The Financial Management Initiative. Report by the Comptroller and Auditor General, (1986), HMSO, London.

The Financial Management Initiative, Thirteenth Report by the Public Accounts Committee, (1987), Session 1986-87, HC 61, HMSO, London.

Part II

Case Studies

Chapter 5

Performance Indicators for Higher Education and Research

Martin Cave and Stephen Hanney

'Something resembling a cargo cult seems to have grown up around
the notion of PIs, so that all manner of power and virtues are ascribed
to them and expectations aroused that by collecting and using them
great benefits will miraculously result'. (Australian Vice-Chancellor's Committee/Australian Committee of Directors and Principals,
1988.)

Expenditures on higher education (HE) and research represent a small
but controversial component of overall public spending. Measuring their
outputs has thus attracted considerable attention from those concerned
both with funding the sector and with spending the allocations. Because
the returns to such expenditures are often intangible and remote in time,
it has been necessary to develop new procedures for measuring output.
Finally, as with other areas of public spending, there are now plans to
introduce more competition and market-type relationships into both HE
and research; these have changed or will change the role of output and
performance measures.

This chapter gives a combined account of the development of Performance Indicators (PIs) for Higher Education (HE) and research, because
of the many overlapping factors affecting both areas. A proportion of the
nation's research budget is spent in HE institutions (HEIs) and more
progress has been made in devising PIs for research activities in HE than
for teaching. Furthermore, one factor in the spread of PIs is the development of new techniques of counting research output and citations, and the
same bibliometric methods may be appropriate for HEIs and for Research
Council institutes. If PIs are to be successfully introduced, they need to
be considered within a proper framework which includes models of the
HE or research system, and such models will have several common

features. This chapter sets out several possible frameworks and gives an account of the context of the development of PIs. It also discusses how they can be used at various levels and how their use changes with the management context.

Frameworks and Models

When a system of PIs is being devised a proper framework for analysis will help reduce dangers. Mayston (1985) showed, on the basis of early American experience, that if PIs lack 'decision relevance', they are ignored. Alternatively, as Chapter 8 demonstrates in the case of local authorities, the introduction of PIs may have an impact, but a dysfunctional one. It could lead to less easily measured activities being given lower priority and it may affect in unanticipated ways the pattern of working relationships between decision-making units and individuals within the organisation, relationships with clients and sponsor, the responsiveness of an organisation to the demands made upon it, and the scope for discretion in the use of resources.

Within the field of HE and research these dangers can be illustrated by a number of examples:

(a) the greater emphasis being given in universities to research, where PIs already operate, than to teaching (Harris, 1986);

(b) a change in the pattern of publications (Cabinet Office, 1989);

(c) the greater pressure to publish, irrespective of the state of the material;

(d) the greater emphasis given to types of research where performance can be measured bibliometrically, at the expense of other objectives.

The Chairman of the Advisory Board for the Research Councils (ABRC), Sir David Phillips, recently underlined the dangers. He retold the story of the drunk explaining to a passer-by that he was looking for his wallet under a street lamp. When the passer-by asked 'Did you lose it here?', the drunk replied, 'Oh no, but this is where the light is'. Phillips, who elsewhere had been described as the 'product champion' of bibliometric techniques (Healey et al, 1988),asked whether they set about the evaluation of research using bibliometric techniques 'because there is a very strong light provided by Eugene Garfield (developer of citations analysis) and others, on the number of publications and citations, etc., or do these measures indeed reflect accurately what is happening in science? We must remember that the scientific literature is only a vehicle for knowledge transfer and that publication and citation rates do not provide simple measures of success in achieving the extrinsic goals of science - not even the increase of understanding, let alone social and economic benefit.' (Phillips, 1989, pp. 215 and 265).

Possible Frameworks

Moravcsik (1986) has usefully proposed a 'methodology for finding a methodology' for the assessment of science, though its potential sphere of application is wider. The framework includes:

(a) identifying the relevant objectives of the organisation;

(b) specifying the parts or levels of the system to be analysed and specifying the uses to which the assessment will be put;

(c) listing the PIs to be used;

(d) devising strategies for their application to the organisation and predicting the implications that their application might have.

Possibly, an analysis of the environment of the organisation should come even before a statement of objectives, especially if it is producing several quite different outputs. Ziman (1989) has argued, in the case of HE, that indicators and other evaluative information concerning research performance are of limited value unless the teaching components have been segregated in both input and output measures. He suggests that the operations of the institution need to be modelled, for example by data envelopment analysis, in terms of an underlying production function with several inputs and a number of outputs covering teaching and research. We have outlined this approach elsewhere in the case of higher education (Cave et al, 1988) but it is also applicable to research.

The Production Model

In the production model higher education institutions are viewed as 'production units' in which inputs are converted into outputs. Despite its apparently reductionist nature this approach is useful not only in shedding light on particular techniques, but also in classifying PIs.

The approach is set out schematically in Figure 5.1, in which higher education is seen as a process for transforming inputs (notably of students' time, academics' time, consumables and the services of equipment and buildings) into outputs which can be broadly classified as relating to either teaching or research. The former includes the value-added of all

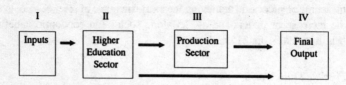

Figure 5.1

those receiving instruction from the university or other higher education institution - undergraduate students, graduate students and those taking short courses. Research is a shorthand for any increase in knowledge generated by the institution, in the form of publications, patents, development work, and the like. Many activities in higher education, notably the preparation of research degrees, combine 'teaching' and 'research' as joint products.

Some higher education outputs are used directly as consumption benefits. For instance, mastery of a discipline or completion of research may yield direct satisfaction. Others are intermediate inputs into other economic processes, or inputs which go back into higher education itself (for simplicity, this feedback is not shown in the diagram). Thus both trained personnel and the results of research are used in all sectors of the economy, including the higher education sector. They are inputs into further transformation processes which generate other outputs, often in the form of consumption goods and services.

The figure thus identifies four points in the overall process at which measures or indicators can be recorded:

(a) inputs;

(b) process or productivity;

(c) intermediate outputs;

(d) final outputs.

In many commercial activities, flows at all of these points would be measurable in money terms, and the measures ultimately be derived from the valuations of output made by final consumers (IV in Figure 5.1). But this approach is not possible within higher education as many of the outputs are difficult or impossible to measure in monetary or even in physical units. Hence the emergence of PIs as partial and approximate 'surrogate' measures either of output or, in many cases, of inputs. Before developing a categorisation of PIs for comparative purposes, it is useful to review two more ambitious techniques of measurement.

Technical Approaches

The first technique to be considered is the explicit calculation of rates of return to investment in higher education, either to society as a whole (the social return) or to the individual student (the private return). The technique first involves computing the teaching-related costs shown in Figure 5.1. These are then compared with the benefits, which are normally estimated as the discounted value of the increments in earnings associated with higher education, although it is difficult to separate these from other background or environmental effects. On fairly stringent assumptions about the operation of labour markets, increments in earnings equal the increments in the value of individuals' marginal product of labour. The calculation thus yields a monetary estimate of the output of higher education derived from the operation of the economy as a whole. Studies of this kind typically distinguish between different disciplines or groups of disciplines (for example social sciences or engineering) and between different levels of degree (for example undergraduate degrees or post-graduate degrees). However, it is not normally possible to distinguish between different institutions of higher education, because of problems of sample size. A similar approach is possible, in principle, in relation to research outputs, but the difficulties of establishing the economic benefits associated with research products rule it out in practice.

Calculation of the returns to higher education have been made for a number of countries, as summarised in Psacharopoulos (1985). One major difficulty with the studies concerns the allocation of costs, in particular the assumption that particular costs can be associated with particular returns. It is extremely difficult to identify, in practice, how, for example, lecturers' time should be divided between teaching and research, and the problem is even more acute in relation to such things as library, computing or administration costs (Clayton, 1987).

An alternative method for comparing inputs and outputs across a range of higher education institutions is data envelopment analysis (DEA), which is discussed in Chapter 2 above. DEA does not require a cost allocation, but unlike cost benefit analysis, which is capable in principle of establishing whether an activity should be undertaken, DEA is only capable of identifying the most efficient method of doing it, and of showing how close to efficiency a particular institution comes. Although some studies of this kind have been done (for examples, see Ahn et al, 1988; Tomkins and Green, 1988), the technique has so far made little impact as its information requirements are high.

PIs in Practice

Both the rate of return method and data envelopment analysis are rigorous but informationally demanding forms of evaluation. In practice, as noted above, performance indicators in higher education have taken the less ambitious route of partial measurement and have involved intercepting flows of inputs or outputs at one of the four stages noted above. For example, the 1986 report of the CVCP/UGC Working Party in the UK distinguished the more conventional categories of input, process and output performance indicators. Input indicators (I in Figure 5.1) have to do with the resources, human and financial, employed by universities. Process indicators (II in Figure 5.1) relate to the intensity or productivity of resource use and to the management effort applied to the inputs or to the operation of the organisation. Output indicators (III and IV in Figure 5.1) concern what has been achieved - the products of the institution. This categorisation is related to but not identical with the distinction familiar in the general literature on performance measurement between economy (reducing the cost of inputs), efficiency (or productivity) and effectiveness (the attainment of objectives) (see for instance Beeton, 1988).

The appropriateness of a production model for HE is not universally accepted (see, for example, Elton, 1988). Some question whether such a static model is entirely relevant for assessing UK investment in the 'science base' or 'core research'. This is a dynamic, exploratory activity with a wide range of outcomes and time scales over which they might be assessed and therefore, it is argued, it might be more appropriate to examine the role of PIs for research within a 'research portfolio - risk and return' model. The Medical Research Council (MRC), for example, refers in its *Corporate Strategy* (1989) to the maintenance of a 'portfolio of investments' which it has to keep in balance by having regard to: demand balance, scientific balance, resource balance, and risk balance. Research projects of differing degrees of risk will require different ways of measuring output, and unless PIs are developed within such a portfolio framework, there may be a tendency to concentrate on those phases of the research cycle when risks are lower and outcomes more measurable.

The Development of PIs for Higher Education and Research

Higher Education

Evaluation and assessment have always been central to the activities of HEIs and, in some respects the development of performance measurement represents a systematisation of existing practices. But, although some PIs were always used in HE they were not systematically applied, and were often perceived as a threat to the traditional and highly valued autonomy of the institution, the department or the individual.

Pioneering work in the conceptual development of specific PIs was conducted in the UK in the late 1970s by John Sizer as part of the OECD's Institutional Management in Higher Education Programme (Sizer, 1979). Further developments at a national level were limited until the Jarratt Report on university efficiency (1985) and the Green Paper on higher education (1985), which recommended the introduction of PIs. In 1986, the Committee of Vice-Chancellors and Principals (CVCP) and the University Grants Committee (UGC) accepted what came to be known as the 'concordat'; if changes in university management requested by the Government, including a development of PIs, were met, further finance would be released to the universities. A joint Working Group was established. The first statement, issued in 1986, consisted of a range of PIs for teaching and research. However, the political pressure was so great that, in the absence of data for many of the desired indicators, the CVCP/UGC published the data that were to hand under the title *University Management Statistics and PIs*. Despite an increase in the number of indicators in the volume from 39 in 1987 to 54 in 1989, most relate to costs. Sizer (1989), a member of the Committee, identifies only two as being output or outcome measures and admits that the set is more useful in assessing efficiency than effectiveness. The limitations of each indicator are explicitly recognised in the publication; in users' hands, however, there is a risk that the indicators are vulnerable to the 'disappearing caveat'.

In 1986, the UGC also published the results of a research selectivity exercise which was used to influence research funding. The extent to which this was based on PIs is contested (Gillett, 1989), but when the exercise was repeated in 1989 it was more systematic and provoked less immediate criticism.

In contrast to this activity in the universities, the public sector has not yet seen the specific development of PIs at a national level. The sector has long had forms of evaluation employed by HMI and the Council for National Academic Awards, but it has been individual institutions that have made the strongest efforts to develop PIs. In 1989, the newly created Polytechnics and Colleges Funding Council (PCFC) established a committee of inquiry on PIs 'to suggest a range of indicators that might be used to assess the performance of institutions and advise how they might be used by the PCFC and the institutions themselves' (PCFC, 1989). In September 1989, the PCFC also commissioned a major study of research.

Many of the reasons for the development of PIs for HE are similar to those behind their development in most public services in the UK: the Government's concern with ensuring value for money, increasing accountability and the strengthening of institutional management. Both in HE and other fields of public policy, these concerns have led to the emergence of what Neave (1988) has termed the 'Evaluative State'. As part of its concern for value for money the Government also stressed the need for quality and this has led to pressures for greater selectivity, especially in research funding. Such pressure has been almost universal, but it has probably been greater in the UK than anywhere else (Cave and Hanney, 1989).

In addition to direct pressure for the introductions of PIs, the cuts made by the UGC in 1981 were criticised for the lack of explicit criteria used, or at least announced. The 1986 research selectivity was also severely criticised (see, for example, Phillimore, 1988 and Smyth and Anderson, 1987 for compilations of the criticisms). But some of the critics have, in effect, been helping to build the case for PIs by arguing that any cut backs or selectivity exercises should be conducted on the basis of open and objective criteria and information.

Research Councils

Although the Government's concentration on value for money and accountability is widely seen as a reason for the development of PIs for the Research Councils (RCs), other factors are also important. In an era of steady state funding, and yet unparalleled growth in scientific opportunities and ever more expensive equipment, emphasis is also placed on the search for more 'objective' decision aids than sole reliance on peer review because the funding decisions become inevitably more controversial (Gibbons and Georghiou, 1987; Ziman, 1987a; Phillips and Turney, 1988). Irvine (1989) suggests that the UK was the first to experience these pressures. Furthermore, in the early 1980s it became apparent that technical developments in bibliometrics might permit policy-relevant use of publication and citation measurement. At that time, the work of Martin and Irvine in analysing the convergence of partial indicators for comparing similar 'big science' facilities attracted wide attention in the UK (Phillips and Turney, 1988, p 192).

As a result of these factors, the ABRC and the Economic and Social Research Council commissioned a series of studies of bibliometric techniques. Each is described in detail in a special edition of the journal *Scientometrics* devoted to developments in the UK (Volume 14, No. 3-4, 1988). The third study produced bibliometric profiles of all publicly financed civil laboratories in the UK.

Developments within the individual RCs have been detailed by Anderson (1989), with the Agricultural and Food Research Council (AFRC) and the Natural Environment Research Council (NERC) taking the lead. This greater progress illustrates the point made earlier about the importance of examining the environment of each organisation. In some respects, the task of developing PIs for the work of researchers in NERC and AFRC institutes is easier than the job of finding PIs for the RC funded work conducted in universities by researchers in receipt of grants from the Science and Engineering Research Council (SERC), or using SERC laboratories for a short period. This is because all the work produced at the institute can be associated with the RC in a way that it cannot for an HEI.

The greater controversy involved in making funding decisions about proposals and institutes at a time of level funding has meant 'there has actually been a demand for quantitative performance data from peer review panels within some agencies and, on at least one occasion, the AFRC discovered that Visiting Group members were, in fact, already conducting their own informal bibliometric analyses of research institutes' (Anderson, 1989, p 110).

In addition to these internal pressures, RCs are facing external pressures to develop PIs from the DES and the Cabinet Assessment Office. The Government's Expenditure White Paper in January 1989 (Treasury, 1989) stated that the DES had developed, through its Working Group on Outputs and Performance Indicators, more than 20 indicators which 'will be used in 1989 to assess progress in meeting the objectives of science policy and the Council's own performance and efficiency targets'. In May 1989 the ABRC listed some of the indicators produced by the RCs in its report to the Secretary of State for the Public Expenditure Survey (ABRC, 1989).

Performance Indicators in Current Use

The full list of PIs now made available by the CVCP/UFC now numbers 54. The discussion below concentrates on analysing several of the important indicators that have been, or could be, introduced; we first consider those used in relation to teaching in HE, then to research in Universities and finally to research councils.

Teaching Indicators

The traditional view was that 'it is extremely difficult to determine how well an academic is carrying out his teaching activities except in cases of serious dereliction of responsibility' (Leverhulme Report, 1983). As recently as 1985, this view was backed by the UGC: 'There are few indicators of teaching performance that would enable a systematic external assessment of teaching quality to be made' (UGC, 22/85). But with resource allocation increasingly linked to research activity there is a danger that all available effort will be diverted to 'grant earning' research activities and teaching will only receive the bare minimum effort. Elton (1987) claimed that 'the UGC decision not to use teaching quality in its resource allocation is inevitably going to lead to a decline in its quality'.

Ministers had been pressing the universities over a long period to give greater attention to teaching quality, and in 1988 the CVCP established a standing group under Professor Sutherland to create an academic standards unit. Following a report from the Sutherland Group on academic audit, a unit has been established. It is proposed, however, that before visiting a university, 'the audit team would *receive* an initial briefing based on performance and other quantitative indicators' (VC/89/160(a)) - (our emphasis). As Sizer argues, however, the unit 'cannot be expected to assess the comparative quality of teaching by subject areas in all universities. There is an important distinction between minimum quality assurance and comparative quality judgements'. Publishable PIs of institutional teaching quality are very difficult to develop (Sizer, 1989, pp 10-15). Apparently, the Joint CVCP/UGC Steering Committee considered possible indicators but concluded that some which are used within institutions, such as classification of honours degrees, are inappropriate for making comparisons between institutions. It took the view that there is a need for universities to undertake formal self-evaluation and appraisal of teaching as a matter of good practice, including the development of systems of individual teacher appraisal and student questionnaires.

We now consider some specific PIs applicable to teaching.

Student Reviews of Teaching

Student reviews of teaching are much more developed in the USA and there are many techniques employed world wide. Two main questions arise: What do they tell us? How could they be used to provide PIs? Murray (1984) gathered considerable evidence from North America and concluded that:

(a) the ratings of a given instructor are reasonably stable;

(b) student ratings correlate reasonably well with ratings made by others;

(c) there is a small but significant correlation with factors such as class size, and severity of gradings;

(d) there is a moderate positive correlation between student ratings of teaching and objective measures of student achievement.

A working party on PIs recommended to the Australian Vice-Chancellors Committee (1988) that student evaluations of teaching and curriculum should be developed in two ways: 'Rating by students on a small number of defined aspects of teaching and of subjects, as indicators of the perceived quality and relevance of teaching and the curriculum; the number of formative evaluations (excluding those done for the overall evaluation) per subject taught and per member of staff in a department as an indicator of commitment to teaching' (AVCC/ACDP, 1988).

Employment of Graduates

The initial report from the CVCP/UGC Working Party suggested that data should be collected after 12 months and five years, but they had to fall back on the First Destination Survey (FDS) because only those figures were available. The Association of Graduate Careers Advisory Services (AGCAS) suggested there were many dangers in using the FDS as a PI, for example, they suggested that the FDS only shows first destinations, not necessarily long term employment patterns. This view is backed by work from Brennan and McGeevor (1988) but Boys and Kirkland (1988) suggest that the FDS is a modest market predictors of success in the labour market over the long term. Taylor (1985) showed that the most important factor in determining different employment rates from different HEIs is the subject mix. The FDS information is used for several PIs in the CVCP/UGC list and the figures take subject mix into account. Taylor and Johnes (1989) examined the value of the FDS as a PI and argued that graduates who were unemployed six months after graduation did have poorer long term career prospects but that there was only limited correlation between the subjects with the highest rates of unemployment after six months and those with the lowest rates of average salary after six years. It can thus be argued that this PI could be used more satisfactorily to compare universities than to compare subjects.

Cost Measures

The CVCP/UGC list is dominated by expenditure items. It is stressed, however, that many of them are management statistics rather than PIs. Several problems emerge: none of the figures on expenditure is broken down between teaching, research and administration, and there is uncertainty about the consistency of measurements across institutions and departments. There is also uncertainty about what may be assumed about the quality of the process and outputs. For example, is a staff:student ratio of 1:10 preferable to one of 1:12; is a high 'library expenditure per FTE student' desirable or something to be concerned about?

Undergraduate Success

Success as a percentage of those ending their studies might be subject to a degree of manipulation, despite the existence of external examiners. This problem may diminish with the development of academic audit.

Qualifications of Full-Time Undergraduate Entrants

This was thought to be important in the 1981 UGC exercise but was not used by the later Working Group on the ground that it is an input, not a performance, measure. However, it now forms indicators 50 to 54. These indicators illustrate a number of points about the importance of relating PIs to objectives. If widening access to HEIs and increasing the age participation rate are important objectives, then a stress on high entry scores could cause some difficulties. A recent report from the Training Agency on widening admissions to HE recommended that 'funding bodies (and especially the UFC) should adopt performance indicators to measure and reward HEIs' success in recruiting - and successfully graduating - applicants with lower A level scores and those with non-traditional qualifications' (Fulton and Ellwood, 1989).

Value-Added

In principle this is an extremely attractive PI, and it was advocated in the 1987 White Paper (DES, 1987). There are several interpretations of what it would entail and what such an indicator might show. The UK thinking often sees it as a comparison of A level entry scores with final degree results. Even this approach is complicated enough because of the uncertainty of the relationship between entry scores and degree results. In America, however, the term embraces a wider range of assessment on entry and exist and there are many practical difficulties (Cave et al, 1988). Furthermore, although the American approach might overcome the objections of narrowness, it would be difficult to use complex value added schemes to compare institutions: 'value added education is tailored to the student characteristics and unique mission of each institution. This promotes the maintenance of diversity in higher education by encouraging varied assessments that avoid inappropriate inter-institutional comparisons.' (Macmillan, 1988).

Indicators for Research in Higher Education

Research Income

In the CVCP/UGC list, research income per member of academic staff is one of only two PIs related to research. It was also used in both the 1986 and 1989 research selectivity exercises. To the extent that ability to generate research income indicates that the research record of a department is thought to be good, then research income is an indicator of performance. Some people claim, however, that research income is an input and that if income is counted as an additional PI along with research output there is double counting.

There is criticism of what is known as the 'Matthew Effect' - 'to him that hath shall be given' (see, for example, Gillett, 1989).

Research Output

The quantity of research output per member of staff was taken into account in the 1989 research selectivity exercise and this was generally thought to be an improvement over 1986. The UFC is expanding the experiment conducted with four subjects to generate a data base of publications and it is intended that this will form part of the CVCP/UGC list. There are many difficulties, including: the different pattern of publications and other research outputs in different subjects; the problem of weighting different types of publications; the treatment of multi-authored works, and perhaps most seriously, the lack of correlation between quantity and quality of output (though a weighting system allows some attention to be given to quality). The UFC appears unlikely to use a weighting system but it will include a wide range of research outputs, and this should overcome some of the problems of different patterns of outputs between subjects (CVCP/UFC, 1989b).

Citations

Although it is possible for the number of citations received by articles in scientific journals to be counted and analysed, there is a considerable dispute about both the meaning of citations and the methods used to count them. A recent compilation of the points was made by Cozzens (1989, p 437). Do they, she asks, 'measure quality, importance, impact, influence, utility, visibility, all of the above, or something else?' The factors that might inflate or reduce citations include: the effects of timing; journal of publication; self-citation; negative citations; whole, fractional or first name counting; in-group citations; language of publication; obliteration by incorporation; field differences; and cross disciplinary citation patterns. There is particular concern about the use of this method in fields outside the natural sciences.

The cost of citation analysis is also considerable, and this, together with the other difficulties, means it is 'open to discussion' whether it is to be used by the CVCP/UFC in its development of quantitative indicators of research to be added to the list of *University Management Statistics and PIs*. In its consultative papers, however, the sub-committee on research indicators noted that the citation analysis undertaken as part of the Oxburgh Report on earth sciences was valuable in adding 'an important additional perspective to the picture produced by the counting of publications.' (CVCP/UFC, 1989b). Furthermore, it recognised that citation analysis is capable of generating a variety of useful measures, including numbers of highly cited papers and uncited papers.

Counts of patents feature in the list of research publications that could be counted. It is also possible for a type of citations analysis to be performed on the papers cited in patent applications and this would help to ensure that applied work is recognised (see, for example, Collins and Wyatt, 1988).

Esteem Indicators

A variety of esteem indicators are being considered by the CVCP/UFC including: membership of learned societies at a level where admission is by competitive election only; major prizes; numbers of visiting scholars supported by formal schemes; journal editorships.

Reputational Rankings

Standing halfway between traditional peer review and bibliometric methods is reputational ranking where the opinion of every head of department, for example, is sought about the other departments in his or her subject. This has been more important in the US for doctoral schools (see, for example, Cartter, 1966 and Roose and Andersen, 1970) than in the UK where the main such rankings for departments were conducted by *The Times Higher Education Supplement*.

PIs for the Research Councils

Most of the research PIs for HEIs appear in the list of PIs being developed for RCs by the DES Working Party. There is even some discussion as to whether the information collected by the CVCP/UFC could be used by RCs (see, for example, Anderson, p 74). The indicators given as an Annexe in the MRC's current Corporate Strategy provide a useful outline of the PIs likely to be developed for the RCs. These PIs are shown in Figure 5.2. Such a list is inevitably an amalgam of input, process and output indicators and as with those for HEIs it serves a variety of purposes including external accountability and improving internal management. Thus PIs for external use might include the extent to which PIs were being applied internally. The 1989 Expenditure White Paper suggested that the PIs being developed were designed to show progress in meeting the Government's objectives for science policy: 'concentration and selectivity of resource use; responsiveness to the needs of industry for research and very highly qualified manpower; the extent to which research is being disseminated and exploited for economic and social benefit; and flexible and efficient management of resources' (Treasury, 1989). There is only space here to make a few selective comments about the indicators. Such comments will often illustrate general points.

Research Output and Impact

Anderson (1989) reviews the considerable work being conducted by RCs to develop, and in some cases use, bibliometric data bases. It is easier to do this for RC institutes than for the publications produced in HEI departments by researchers in receipt of RC grants, although greater efforts are being made for the source of funding to be acknowledged. Anderson suggests (p 117) that publications and citations 'have gained widespread acceptance but more complicated constructs such as "journal influence weights" have met with hostility'. The journal influence weight

Research Output and Impact
    eg publications, patents

Types of Research Activity
    eg expenditure on basic research, collaborative research
    with industry

Concentration and Selectivity in Research Funding
    eg distribution of funding between HEIs

Manpower
    eg numbers of studentships, PhD submission rates

Responsiveness to Needs of Employers
    eg income from private sector

International Activity
    eg number of formal international commitments

Management, Administration and Value for Money
    eg proportion of budget spent on central administration

Flexibility
    eg number of staff on fixed term contracts

Collaboration Between Councils
    eg number and value of Inter-Research Council projects,
    programmes and centres

(Source: MRC Corporate Strategy, 1989)

Figure 5.2: Performance Indicators for Research Councils

technique was used in the ABRC commissioned study of all scientific HEIs departments and civil laboratories (see Carpenter et al, 1988). This study, partly because of the criticism of the 1986 UGC selectivity exercise, used the average number of citations that articles in a journal receive. It is cheaper than full citations analysis and can be conducted as soon as articles have been published, but it is not as precise and McGinnety (1988) describes in a study for NERC how the scaling of journal or influence weights is intuitively disturbing to environmental scientists. For bibliometric methods used by RCs Anderson concludes that 'attempts to rely solely on data from publicly available sources such as bibliographic data bases have, on the whole, proved less successful than when emphasis is placed on the direct collection of data from scientists' (p 117). Work on citations in the social sciences has been conducted for the ESRC including some by Roberts on citations from the work of postgraduate students.

Types of Research Activity

The inclusion of level of collaboration with industry and income from the private sector illustrates potential problems unless the list of PIs is developed with flexibility. Whilst collaboration with industry is a very important objective of research, for much of the research funded by the ESRC, and others, collaboration with and gaining additional income from the public sector is equally important.

Concentration and Selectivity in Research Funding

One possible indicator under this heading would be the ratio of programmes to project grants, with the aim of illustrating the extent to which the objective of shifting balance of support more towards programmes had been met. Another PI used in the 1989 ABRC Report was average size of grant, which had risen from £38K in 1987 to £50K in 1988. These examples usefully illustrate the care needed when using PIs to show effectiveness because, in fact, the data bases being developed by the RCs, for example, AFRC, NERC and ESRC, will be able to achieve the task of comparing 'the quality of research funded through grants and initiatives' (ESRC, Corporate Plan, 1988). It is this that would indicate how far the policy impacts meet the policy aims. A similar debate rages over the desirability of concentrating research into large laboratories (see, for example, Ziman, 1989; Hare and Wyatt, 1988) and therefore the role of PIs in showing effectiveness in this field is complex.

Manpower

First destination and longer term employment experience could provide useful PIs although there are difficulties as with the FDS for graduates. The PhD submission rate can be used as a PI for a variety of purposes but again there might be legitimate differences between RCs. Ziman (1987b), for example, claims that the research process for a social science PhD differs from that for a natural science one and it is therefore likely to take longer to complete.

Management, Administration and Value for Money

As with all PIs there are dangers of manipulation and it is important to allow for differences between expenditure patterns of RCs (i.e. size of the average project) and the sensitivity of the results to accounting conventions. Thus, some administrative costs can be attributed either to the RC or to research institutions and in that way be counted as research rather than administrative costs.

Policy Usefulness

There is considerable interest in seeing whether PIs can be developed to illustrate the economic and social impact of research (see for example, Gibbons and Georghiou, 1987). Measuring policy usefulness is especially important for the ESRC, with its first objective (Corporate Plan, 1988. para 4.2) being 'to support a programme of high-quality research in the social sciences, which produces new knowledge, advances research techniques and provides information of value to policy makers'. It is very difficult to develop quantifiable PIs that go much beyond measuring the amount of media coverage etc. given to research reports to show this. Nevertheless, indicators that encourage researchers to identify their clientele and ensure that results are disseminated will link in with the approach adopted by the largest charitable supporters of social science research, the Rowntree Trust.

One possible way forward would be to interview some of the people for whom the research is intended about its usefulness in furnishing policy - relevant information and analysis. There are great problems in converting such evaluations into PIs but the process is akin to the efforts being made to develop PIs from peer and student review of university departments. More generally, it should be possible to scrutinise key policy developments and identify any contributions of research. The difficulties include the danger of manipulation through collusion and the difficulty of making comparisons across programmes with a different composition of user groups. It is important to analyse the possible models of how research influences policy makers and practitioners (see, for example, Bulmer, 1987 and Husen and Kogan, 1984) and, in particular, to consider the complexities involved when Government Departments commission research and/or carry out the research in their institutes (Kogan and Henkel, 1983).

Other Examples of PIs of Research

The technique developed by Martin and Irvine (see, for example, 1983) of using 'converging partial indicators' to examine 'Big Science' fields including radioastronomy and high energy physics have been extremely influential yet controversial (see, for example, the debate in *Social Studies in Science*, 1985). In addition to publications, citation counts and number of highly cited papers, this method uses direct evaluation based upon interviews with peers. Irvine and Martin have been recognised as world leaders in the application of such techniques (Irvine, 1989; Shadish, 1989).

PIs of research have featured in a plan for a full development of PIs for a whole museum (Bud et al, 1990) and as part of an evaluation of the research of a museum (Georghiou, 1989). In both cases, the number of outside requests for assistance has been used in addition to bibliometric approaches.

Across the board in R and D Assessment, PIs are recognised as having a place but the recent guide from the Cabinet Office (1989, p 42) concludes that bibliometric methods, 'are valuable to supplement peer review but not yet mature enough to replace it'.

The Impact of Performance Indicators

We noted at the outset that PIs can have negligible or even adverse effects if used outside a proper frame of reference. It is also clear that most PIs or sets of PIs for higher education and research are vulnerable to serious objections related to their ability to capture adequately the true desired outcomes of the activities in question.

It is thus useful to recall Klein and Carter's (1988) valuable distinction between the use of PIs as 'dials' or as 'tin openers'. If they are the former, measuring accurately the inputs, outputs and processes of the 'black box' of HE or research, they can be used directly to regulate the supply of resources. If they are the latter, their function is to identify issues requiring further examination and to act as an aid to judgement. According to this view, PIs play a role in increasing the transparency and accountability of judgmental decision taking by superior bodies, and at the same time they can be integrated into management systems which make subordinate organisations more accountable for attainment *ex post* of performance objectives.

The fallibility of output measures applicable to higher education and research makes the 'tin opener' approach inevitable within the present management framework. Applying PIs directly in resource allocation could also be challenged on the ground that it was directing marginal resources on the basis of data on average returns - a procedure which is unlikely to promote allocative efficiency.

This does not rule out improvements in the composition of the PIs. Carter (1989) has remarked that PIs in the UK have been 'data-driven': that is, they are based on available data rather than on information gathered for the specific purposes of constructing a relevant measure. As time passes this criticism become gradually less applicable, as new data sets are constructed which make possible consistent comparisons across institutions or over time. That process has been seen in the expansion of PIs collected for universities. But it is also reflected in criticism that excessive resources are being devoted to such evaluation (£4 million, for instance, was spent on carrying out the UFC's research appraisals in 1989).

But using PIs as an aid to judgement raises a 'weighting' problem: how much weight should be given to the numbers and how much to judgements, especially in cases where the two diverge? Equally, the choice of comparator used to evaluate performance (for instance, past performance of the same unit or the performance of a set of equivalent units) may influence interpretation of the PIs.

In practice, the weighting problem within funding and research councils and in institutions themselves is often resolved in favour of judgement, but the additional data made available can influence and sometimes justify the judgement. As a consequence, collection and presentation of PIs need not always strengthen the hand of managers and information collators: the effect is sometimes, paradoxically, to strengthen the role of professional judgement rather than to weaken it. This outcome is noted by Anderson (1989) in the case of several research councils. A similar outcome may arise in higher education - for instance in the UFC's 1989 research selectivity exercise where final judgements were made by expert sub-committees and were to some degree protected from criticism by the data collection exercise which preceded them, despite problems with that exercise which the UFC itself acknowledges (UFC, 1989a).

The weight to be given to expert judgement and the importance of errors and ambiguities in the measures vary with the level at which the data are used. Within the framework of managing higher education, at least five levels of use can be discerned: in dialogues between the Treasury and the Department of Education and Science, between the DES and the funding bodies, between the funding bodies and institutions, within institutions, and within departments.

Most of the discussion in this chapter has concentrated upon the lower level uses. But it is unlikely that simple aggregation of indicators used there would make them appropriate for higher level discussions. For instance, the annual CVCP/UFC publication, *University Management Statistics and Performance Indicators* relies for its value on comparisons with other universities. Aggregation across all universities - for instance, for comparison with PCFC institutions - is not practicable at present, because of the procedures used.

The need for highly aggregative output measures to be used in upper level discussions is becoming more acute as more data will shortly be made available about the split in university funding between allocations for teaching and research. Once this information is public knowledge the DES will have to justify its split of funds for teaching between the UFC and PCFC and for research between higher education institutions and research councils. Indicators for these purposes are still in an early stage of development, hampered by the lack of natural comparators. At the same time, existing performance indicators in use at the lower levels of the management process - in discussions between the funding bodies and institutions, and within institutions - are also likely to come under intensified pressure for reasons related to changes in funding arrangements.

A similar diversity of use can be seen in the case of PIs for RCs which can be employed both externally for accountability and as part of the Public Expenditure Survey exercise, and internally to strengthen the management and enhance the efficiency of RCs. Furthermore, showing externally that PIs are being used internally is one way of illustrating the RC's commitment to increasing value for money. A PI for research training, the percentage of PhDs submitted within four years, illustrates the various possible uses of PIs and levels of application. It has been used by RCs to compare departments or HEIs. The ESRC, for example, chose to use the PI as a dial and denied automatically studentships to poor performers. It may also be used to show comparative figures and provide a total picture of the performance of RCs. This is how it was used in the 1989 Expenditure White Paper which showed the ESRC in a poor light. But the 1989 ABRC Report correctly recognised the danger of disappearing caveats when PIs are used to compare RCs. It pointed out that performance should be compared to previous performance and to targets and in this way showed that the ESRC had improved its performance. The submission rates PI can also be used as a 'tin opener' as SERC have shown. Their figures revealed that there was a low submission rate for engineering postgraduates, and this raised questions about whether engineering PhDs were meeting the needs of industry.

Bibliometric PIs are increasingly being used as part of *ex post* evaluation of RC institutes by Visiting Groups, and of programmes and research centres within HEI by RC committees. Such use is still highly controversial (see, for example, Ziman, 1989a). There is a danger of manipulation, and Anderson shows the value of the provision of 'coaching' for Visiting Group members which is sometimes provided by the evaluation officials responsible for collecting and analysing the data. He also shows that such PIs are used as 'tin openers' by Visiting Groups to RC institutes and enable them to ask more detailed questions: 'indicators have undoubtedly helped to raise hard questions and force answers, so preventing the peer review process from becoming too soft... where the judgement of reviewers contradicted the evidence of the indicator data, the reviewers may have greater onus on them to justify their position.' (p 115).

Whilst bibliometric PIs have been most readily applied to *ex post* evaluations, they could also have a role in *ex ante* choices the fields of research for concentration and in considering applicants for individual grants. The consideration of appropriate PIs can help in the setting of objectives for an organisation and they can be seen to have several roles in relation to the corporate planning procedure of RCs. They can help establish priority areas for research, and they can also be included in a RC's Corporate Plan as a way of showing how progress towards achieving targets can be monitored. Anderson lists 47 indicators proposed by SERC to monitor implementation of the recommendations in the 1989 Corporate Plan. Clearly many of these are not quantitative PIs.

If the traditional system of management of HE and research seems to offer PIs a subordinate though expanding role, reforms in the overall system of management of higher education and research could alter the position.

At the risk of caricature, two extreme forms of organisation of higher education and research can be distinguished - a fully centralised system in which institutions receive instructions and have little decision-taking flexibility, and a market-based system in which students and other customers exercise consumer choice. In many countries there is a move towards an indirectly centralised system in which institutions are increasingly guided to respond to centrally-established incentives or to compete for private and public funds through a quasi-competitive process. Thus several countries, including the UK, are moving towards a more market-based framework though a system of competitive contracting for some student places. PIs play a vital role in this type of system, not only as a way of making institutions accountable and allocations transparent but also as a mechanism for defining the nature of the academic 'product' for which contracts are made. Hence the new pre-occupation with measures of teaching quality.

The Polytechnics and Colleges Funding Council is currently undertaking a procedure which the UFC will copy in which institutions bid for a number of student places in terms of price per student (UFC, Circular 39/89). The outcome is thus a quasi-auction or competitive tendering system which seeks to use the price mechanism to co-ordinate the demand for student places in different disciplines with the number which institutions are prepared to supply.

The outcome of this process of competitive contracting depends upon the detailed rules of the game - the proportion of student places allocated in this way, the institution's capacity to offer complicated price schedules, etc. But clearly any such contract must include a specification of quality, with the attendant risk that the institution might exploit any errors or omissions in the quality indicators employed.

Because the institutions' relationship with the funding councils is a long term one, they are unlikely to seek to maximise short term gains. But clearly the new system imposes rather different strains on performance indicators of quality than the present ones, and this has worried the institutions. It remains to be seen whether quantitative PIs or monitoring and inspection procedures can be developed which will carry the weight required of them in the new system of higher education funding or can cope with possible similar extensions to the field of research.

References

Advisory Board for the Research Councils, (1989), *Science and Public Expenditure 1989*, DES, London.

Ahn, T., Arnold, V., Charnes, A., Cooper, W. W., (1988), 'Some Statistical and DEA Evaluations of Relative Efficiencies of Public and Private Institutions of Higher Learning', *Socio-Economic Planning Sciences*, 6, 259-269.

Anderson, J., (1989), *New Approaches to Evaluation in UK Research Funding Agencies*, Science Policy Support Group, London.

Australian Vice-Chancellor's Committee, Australian Committee of Directors and Principals, (1988), *Report of the AVCC/ACDP Working Party on Performance Indicators*, Canberra.

Beeton, D., (ed), (1988), *Performance Measurement:: Getting the Concept Right*, Public Finance Foundation, London.

Boys, C. and Kirkland, J., (1988), *Degrees of Success: Career Aspirations and Destinations of Graduates*, Jessica Kingsley Publishers, London.

Brennan, J., and McGeevor, P., (1988), *Graduates at Work*, Jessica Kingsley Publishers, London.

Bud, R., Cave, M., Hanney, S., (1990), *Measuring the Output of Museums*, Mimeo.

Bulmer, M., (ed), (1987), *Social Science Research and Government*, Cambridge University Press.

Cabinet Office, (1989), *Research and Development Assessment: A Guide for Customers and Managers of R and D*, HMSO, London.

Carpenter, M., Gibb, F., Harris, M., Irvine, J., Martin, B., Narin, F., (1988), 'Bibliometric Profiles for British Academic Institutions: An Experiment to Develop Research Output Indicators', *Scientometrics*, 14, 213-233.

Carter, N., (1989), 'Performance Indicators: 'Backseat Driving' or 'Hands Off' Control?', *Policy and Politics*, 17, 131-8.

Cartter, A., (1966), *An Assessment of Quality in Graduate Education*, American Council of Education.

Cave, M., Hanney, S., Kogan, M., Trevett, G., (1988), *The Use of Performance Indicators in Higher Education*, Jessica Kingsley Publishers, London.

Cave, M., and Hanney, S., (1989), *Performance Indicators in Higher Education: An International Survey*, Department of Economics Discussion Paper, Brunel University.

Clayton, K., (1987), *The Measurement of Research in Higher Education*, University of East Anglia.

Collins, P., Wyatt, S., (1988), 'Citations in Patents to the Basic Research Literature', *Research Policy*, 17, 65-74.

Committee of Vice-Chancellors and Principals/University Grants Committee, (1986), *Performance Indicators in Universities*, First Statement of the Joint CVCP/UGC Working Group, CVCP, London.

Committee of Vice-Chancellors and Principals/Universities Funding Council, (1989a), *University Management Statistics and Performance Indicators*, CVCP/UFC, London.

Committee of Vice-Chancellors and Principals/Universities Funding Council, (1989b), *Issues in Quantitative Assessment of Departmental Research*, UFC, London.

Cozzens, S., (1989), 'What Do Citations Count? The Rhetoric-First Model', *Scientometrics*, 15, 437-447.

Crewe, I., (1987), *Reputation, Research and Reality: The Publication Records of UK Departments of Politics 1978-1984*, Essex Papers in Politics and Government, No. 44, Department of Government, University of Essex.

Department of Education and Science, (1987), *Higher Education: Meeting the Challenge*, White Paper, Cm. 114, HMSO.

Economic and Social Research Council, (1988), *Corporate Plan 1989-1994*, ESRC, Swindon.

Elton, L., (1987), 'UGC Resource Allocation and the Assessment of Teaching Quality', *Higher Education Review*, 19, 9-17.

Elton, L., (1988), Book Review, *Studies in Higher Education*, 23, 337-8.

Fulton, O., Ellwood, S., (1989), *Admissions to Higher Education: Policy and Practice*, The Training Agency.

Georghiou, L., (1989), 'Organisation of Evaluation', in Evered, D., Harnett, S., (eds), *The Evaluation of Scientific Resarch*, Wiley, Chichester (CIBA Foundation Conference).

Gibbons, M., and Georghiou, L., (1987), *Evaluation of Research: A Selection of Current Practices*, OECD, Paris.

Gillett, R., (1989), 'Research Performance Indicators Based on Peer Review: A Critical Analysis', *Higher Education Quarterly*, 43, 20-38.

Green Paper, (1985), *The Development of Higher Education into the 1990s*, HMSO, Cmnd 9524, London.

Hare, P., Wyatt, G., (1988), 'Modelling the Determination of Research Output in British Universities', *Research Policy*, 17, 315-329.

Harris, M., (1986), *Judgements of Quality in Higher Education: The Role of the University Grants Committee*, Paper presented to the Anglo-American Seminar on Quality and Judgements in Higher Education at Templeton College.

Healey, P., Irvine, J., Martin, B., (1988), 'Scientometrics Research in the United Kingdom', *Scientometrics*, 14.

Irvine, J., (1989), 'Evaluation of Scientific Institutions: Lessons from a Bibliometric Study of UK Technical Universities', in Evered, D., and Harnett, S., (eds), *The Evaluation of Scientific Research*, Wiley, Chichester (CIBA Foundation Conference).

Jarratt Report, (1985), *Report of the Steering Committee for Efficiency Studies in Universities*, Committee of Vice-Chancellors and Principals, London.

Klein, R., and Carter, N., (1988), 'Performance Measurement: A Review of Concepts and Issues', in Beeton, D., (ed), *Performance Measurement: Getting the Concepts Right*, Public Finance Founcation.

Kogan, M., and Henkel, M., (1983), *Government and Research*, Heinemann Educational Books.

Martin, B., and Irvine, J., (1983), 'Assessing Basic Research: Some Partial Indicators of Scientific Progress in Radio Astronomy', *Research Policy*, 12, 61-90.

Mayston, D., (1985), 'Non-Profit Performance Indicators in the Public Sector', *Financial Accountability and Management*, 1, 51-74.

McMillan, J., (1988), 'Beyond Value-Added Education', *Journal of Higher Education*, 59, 564-579.

McGinnety, J., (1988), 'The Natural Environment Research Council (NERC): Recent Experiences with Quantitative Science Policy Studies', *Scientometrics*, 14, 283-294.

Medical Research Council, (1989), *Corporate Strategy*, MRC, London.

Moravcsik, M., (1986), 'Assessing the Methodology for Finding a Methodology for Assessment', *Social Studies of Science*, 26, 534-39.

Murray, H., (1984), 'The Impact of Formative and Summative Evaluation of Teaching in North American Universities', *Assessment and Evaluation in Higher Education*, 11, 117-29.

Neave, G., (1988), 'On the Cultivation of Quality, Efficiency and Enterprise: An Overview of Recent Trends in Higher Education in Western Europe, 1986-1988', *European Journal of Education*, 23, 7-23.

Phillimore, A., (1989), 'University Research Performance Indicators in Practice: The University Grants Committee's Evaluation of British Universities 1985-6', *Research Policy*, 18, 255-71.

Phillips, D., and Turney, J., (1988), 'Bibliometrics and UK Science Policy', *Scientometrics*, 14, 185-200.

Phillips, D., (1989), 'Chairman's Remarks', in Evered, D., Harnett, S., (eds), *The Evaluation of Scientific Research*, Wiley, Chichester (CIBA Foundion Conference).

Polytechnics and Colleges Funding Council, (1989), *Press Release: Committee of Inquiry on Performance Indicators*, PCFC, London, 6.6.89.

Psacharopoulos, G., (1985), 'Returns to Education: A Further International Update and Implications', *Journal of Human Resources*, 4, 583-604.

Roose, K., and Andersen, A., (1970), *A Rating of Graduate Programs*, American Council on Education.

Shadish, W., (1989), 'Science Evaluation: A Glossary of Possible Contents', *Social Epistemology*, 3, 189-204.

Sizer, J., (1979), 'Assessing Institutional Performance: An Overview', *International Journal of Institutional Management in Higher Education*, 3, 49-77.

Sizer, J., (1989), *Performance Indicators and Quality Control in Higher Education*, Keynote Address to an International Conference, Institute of Education, London.

Smyth, F., and Anderson, J., (1987), *University Performance Indicators*, Science Policy Support Group Aide-Memoire No. 1, SPSG, London.

Taylor, J., (1985), *Comparing Universities: Some Observations on the First Destinations of New Graduates*, University of Lancaster, Discussion Paper.

Taylor, J., Johnes, J., (1989), 'An Evaluation of Performance Indicators Based upon the First Destination of University Graduates', *Studies in Higher Education*, 14, 201-217.

Tomkins, C. and Green, R., (1988), 'Experiments in the Use of Data Envelopment Analysis for Evaluating the Efficiency of UK Accounting Departments', *Financial Accountability and Management*, 4, 147-164.

Treasury, *The Government's Expenditure Plans 1989/90 to 1991/92*, (1989), Chapter 12, Cm. 612, HM Treasury, London.

Universities Funding Council, (1989a), *Report on the 1989 Research Assessment Exercise*.

University Grants Committee, (1985), *Circular Letter 22/85*.

Universities Funding Council, (1989), *Circular Letter 39/89*.

Ziman, J., (1987), *Science in a Steady State: The Research System in Transition*, Science Policy Support Group, London.

Ziman, J., (1987b), 'Social and Natural Science PhDs Compared', *ESRC Newsletter*, 60.

Ziman, J., (1989), *Restructuring Academic Science: A New Framework for UK Policy*, Science Policy Support Group, London.

Ziman, J., (1989a), 'Shelf Life', *The Times Higher Education Supplement*, 1.9.89.

Chapter 6

Performance and Outcome Measures in the Health Service

Helen Roberts

This paper is concerned with approaches to measuring performance and assessing process and outcomes in health services and with how they relate to health service objectives. This is obviously a very wide field and the work which is developing in the UK is not comprehensive. The paper selects a number of key areas in which progress is being made at present. The key areas fall into three categories: work related to process; work related to outcome; and work related to performance. In the field of process it looks at medical audit and patient satisfaction. The next section looks at the measurement of outcomes including perioperative deaths and quality adjusted life years. Finally, in the section on performance, which links outputs to inputs, NHS performance indicators are reviewed. The paper concludes with a look at possible developments in the context of the changes to the NHS announced in the 1989 White Paper, 'Working for Patients', (Department of Health, 1989), which seeks to increase competition in the NHS by moving in the direction of a market system.

Objectives and Approaches

Definitions and Objectives

The general reasons for being interested in performance of the health services and health outcomes are clear: to establish in aggregate whether we are getting value from expenditure on health services and whether those services are effective. But this general aim obscures a number of separate issues which need to be disentangled, such as the definition of health and the objectives of the health services.

There is no single, much less simple, answer to the question 'what is health?'. Definitions range from the medical model which defines health negatively as 'absence of disease' to more positive definitions based on capacity or function. The standard positive and holistic definition of health is that promulgated by the World Health Organisation. WHO defines health as 'a state of optimal physical, mental and social well-being and not merely the absence of disease or infirmity'. WHO also regards health as a fundamental human right and calls for the political commitment of the State as part of its strategy for 'Health for All by the Year 2000' (WHO, 1978).

Objectives of health services are usually set in very general terms such as 'promoting length and quality of life', rather than in operational terms. Indeed, it has been a criticism of the very broad definition of health adopted by the WHO that it cannot effectively be translated into operational objectives. Nevertheless, the WHO has attempted to set targets for the WHO European region; the 38 targets for the year 2000 include:

- By the year 2000, the average number of years that people live free from major disease and disability should be increased by at least 10%

- By the year 2000, there should be no indigenous measles, poliomyelitis, neonatal tetanus, congenital rubella, diphtheria, congenital syphilis or indigenous malaria in the region

- By the year 2000, life expectancy at birth in the region should be at least 75 years

- By the year 2000, infant mortality in the region should be less than 20 per 1,000 live births

The objectives of the NHS, however, are less clearly established. The 1989 Public Expenditure White Paper (HM Treasury, 1989) sets out the aims and objectives of the NHS as follows:

'The NHS aims to improve and promote health and to provide necessary treatment for illness and care while making the best use of available resources. In meeting these objectives the NHS needs to:

- take advantage of advances in clinical treatment and practice;

- improve its response to the consumer;

- give increasing prominence to the promotion of good health and the prevention of illness.'

The Government's objectives for the NHS are also set out in the White Paper 'Working for Patients' (Department of Health, 1989) and are:

'to give patients, wherever they live in the UK, better health care and greater choice of the services available; and greater satisfaction and rewards for those working in the NHS who successfully respond to local needs and preferences'.

In the UK there are no clear detailed targets across the NHS as a whole, although there are some centrally defined targets, for levels of immunisation by GPs, for example. The Government appears to view the setting of such targets as a local responsibility, but has not defined operationally the overarching objectives of the NHS.

Approaches to Assessing Health Services

The simplest model of health services is one analogous to that of the firm as producer in neoclassical economics. Regarding the NHS as a supplier of health care in response to patient demand leads to a view of the system as a production process, analogous to that set out for higher education and research at pp 61 to 63 above. This leads to an economics-based classification of different stages in the process of health care:

- inputs to the process, including patients, clinicians and nurses, buildings and equipment and other staff.

- intermediate outputs or throughputs, i.e. what happens to the patient and the system of care during the treatment process before discharge.

- outputs or the patients as they emerge from the treatment process.

- outcomes of health care or the status of the patient in the long term, e.g. the length and quality of life.

This is a useful taxonomy but inevitably it is oversimplified: in particular the distinction between outputs and outcomes may not always be watertight and some short term outputs (e.g. death of patient) are also outcomes. Moreover this taxonomy does not provide a methodology or approach to assessing health. One influential approach is that suggested by Donabedian (1980) consisting of three (simultaneous) approaches to assessing the quality of care:

- structure, or 'the relatively stable characteristics of the providers of care, of the tools and resources they have at their disposal, and the physical and organisational settings in which they work';

- process, or 'the set of activities which go on within and between the practitioners and patients': this is the focus of assessment, but the basis of assessment of quality is the consequences of that process to the health and welfare of individuals and society;
- outcomes or 'a change in a patient's current and future health status that can be attributed to antecedent health care', taking health status quite broadly to include social and psychological functions as well as patient attitudes.

This yields a structure/ process/ outcome framework for assessing health systems. For structure, the approach depends on the influence of structure on care: structural features known to have a good effect on care are taken as evidence of good quality and vice versa - so structure 'is rather a blunt instrument', only indicating 'general tendencies'. There is little specific information about structure of health services available in this form, and it seems that reliable assessments depend on a thorough analysis of the other aspects: process and outcomes. This paper therefore takes an approach to assessment based on process and outcomes both for the health service in aggregate and looking at specific sub-systems or units. It looks at initiatives underway in the NHS relevant to these.

Process is defined as being inside the black box of production in the NHS. Given a set of inputs we are concerned with how these are processed, for example within a hospital or by a GP or in the system for delivering community care. The focus of activity is to improve the functioning, efficiency and quality of delivery systems. The relevant areas considered in the rest of this report are: medical audit, and patient satisfaction.

But looking at outcomes involves taking a broader and longer term view. Outcomes must be related to the reasons for and objectives of health care systems: for example, one clear (though highly aggregated) outcome measure is life expectancy. One would expect analysis of (long term) outcomes to feed back into fundamental decisions about the balance of resource allocation between different approaches to cure/care within the health sector. Donabedian's proposal for outcomes assessment highlighted one inevitable difficulty: because outcomes generally concern longer term consequences many factors other than the health care activity can intervene and it will be difficult (though necessary) to indicate the causal link between health care and outcome, so that consequences are attributable to that activity. On outcomes, his paper looks at the quality adjusted life year (QALY) methodology, studies of short term clinical outcomes, and outcomes connected with perioperative deaths.

In addition to looking at general questions of assessing process and outcomes for which a partial approach - at best - is available at present, the paper also addresses more practical developments which seek to relate inputs to outputs along the lines of the producer model. Thus performance encompasses both inputs and outputs. This is not always straightforward. There may be no clear line at the end of a process which defines 'outputs'. Similarly the borderline between output and outcomes will often be blurred. This definition of performance is closely concerned with efficiency. On performance this chapter reviews progress with the Department of Health's performance indicators.

Process Evaluation

Medical Audit

Medical audit is basically about quality assurance within the medical profession; taking a wider definition, say, clinical audit, would bring in other professions but it is instructive to focus on medical practice. The Government's White Paper, 'Working for Patients' (Department of Health, 1989) defines medical audit as the 'systematic, critical analysis of the quality of medical care, including the procedures used for diagnosis and treatment, the use of resources, and the resulting outcome and quality of life for the patient.' As well as the concern to go beyond process and embrace outcomes, a key question in relation to medical audit is how effectively it links to other activities to promote quality, effectiveness or value for money within the health care system. This section reviews activity in the UK and other countries and looks at the potential contribution to improving process in health care.

There is no watertight definition of medical audit as the generality of the White Paper definition above indicates. It focuses on peer review by clinicians both locally and at a national level; and its broad objective is quality assurance. An important feature of medical audit is that it should be a process which involves evaluation of performance and feedback to practitioners. And it should be a developing rather than a static process if it is to be effective.

There are a number of reasons why medical audit is now generally seen as a necessary development and has been highlighted in the White Paper. One important reason is to reduce the high cost of 'not getting it right first time' and of inappropriate treatment. Reducing errors should also improve effectiveness of resource use by reducing opportunity costs, and should improve outcomes. Medical audit should also improve clinical accountability in the NHS, and focus clinical attention on the need to satisfy patients as consumers. But although the benefits are potentially significant, the costs in clinical time, information and other resources are high. At present, medical audit is largely an act of faith rather than based on demonstrable benefits. An important aspect is that medical audit if effective should change the practice and behaviour of clinicians, and as with any organisational change this will take a number of years to achieve.

Medical audit or clinical review is also important for management. It can identify process variations which would not otherwise be visible. These include the use of unnecessary materials, the inappropriate use of services in automatic reattendances, number of in-patient days spent waiting for treatment, inappropriate admissions or care which is of no direct value to the patient concerned. All of these potentially increase the information base for management to judge performance and allocate resources. But this does not mean that the audit process and its products should be 'owned', planned or controlled by management. A key question in seeking to establish a system of medical audit is the role of management. Irrespective of this, management support for establishing a medical audit system is crucial, and some means of accountability to management inevitable - however aggregated.

It is worth considering an example of medical audit and its benefits in practice. The Lothian work provides one of the best examples of evaluation of audit in the UK and the link of audit to outcomes (Gruer et al.,1986). The Lothian approach was a relatively straightforward system which integrated data on operations and deaths into routine clinical recording and reviewed the data annually. Over five years significant improvements in performance were recorded; e.g. falling reoperation rate for postoperative complications, and transferring cases requiring emergency treatment of abdominal aortic aneurysms from generalist to specialist surgeons more than doubled the survival rate (Devlin, 1988). Though it cannot be proven that this was due to the audit, those involved believed audit an important factor and particularly praised its simplicity. Thus audit brought other benefits such as a shift in clinical specialisation over time.

The Government is clearly committed to medical audit. It believes that every doctor should participate in regular systematic medical audit; that the system should be medically led and that the overall form of audit should be agreed locally. It describes management's responsibility as that of ensuring that an effective system of medical audit is in place. The aim is to establish a District medical audit advisory committee by April 1991 to include doctors representing the District General Manager (DGM). The committee will then plan and monitor a comprehensive programme of medical audit to be agreed with the DGM; the Government's approach is thus to let audit develop locally.

It seems likely that consistent efforts to establish medical audit machinery will have a beneficial effect, though the cost in time and resources should not be underestimated. Even if the resulting medical audit practices are dynamic and developing it will take several years for benefits to flow.

Patient Satisfaction

Work on patient satisfaction seeks to give the consumer - the patient and his or her relatives - a voice on the quality of health care. By obtaining patients' opinions on different aspects of the treatment process and feeding these back to clinicians, managers and others, the quality of the way in which care is delivered should improve. But patient satisfaction is a complex and elusive target. It is difficult to define because it is clearly a multi-dimensional concept covering a range of concerns such as personal attitudes, quality of technical medical treatment, the continuity of care, the physical environment and the longer term effectiveness of treatment. It is not possible to obtain a global measure of satisfaction because the different aspects are non-commensurate. And crucially there are no existing agreed standards which can form the basis of assessment.

There are a number of reasons why patient satisfaction is of increasing importance in the NHS. The general trends of increasing public sector accountability and consumerism and the right to patient choice are significant. The Griffiths Report on the management of the NHS (Griffiths, 1983) emphasised that the 'experience and perception of patients and the community' were 'central to the approach of management' in ascertaining how well the service is being delivered at local level. Patient satisfaction or acceptability consistently appears in taxonomies of quality. Arguably, patient satisfaction is also one form of outcome measure as well as being central to assessment of process.

There are difficult problems about operationalising patient satisfaction, because of its multi-dimensionality. For example, may not be reliable over time. There can be no check whether patients' answers are consistent. Satisfaction may often depend on the format and length of communication with the patient rather than technical content. A variety of factors may affect patients' satisfaction, for example older people and women express greater satisfaction. And there remains a difficulty of getting patient feedback on the quality of care rather than hotel services.

The major patient satisfaction research exercise in the UK is that being undertaken by CASPE at Bloomsbury Health Authority. It is based on self-completion questionnaires for patients, asking for an index rating (1-4) of each of 15 aspects of services. The questionnaires cover both clinical and non-clinical aspects of care, for example nurses' and doctors' treatment and information on the one hand and physical environment, ward atmosphere, facilities and privacy on the other. The questionnaires are generated automatically from the computerised patient administration system (PAS) when a patient is admitted as an in-patient or booked in as an out-patient. Questionnaires are handed to patients on discharge and returned through the internal hospital post. The completed forms are read by computer and aggregated to give an overall index of satisfaction. Indices can be produced by ward, consultant or any other level and by any topic. The system already applies to the acute and maternity sectors and complementary systems for continuing care, paediatrics and general practice are being developed.

This approach can be linked to the management process by setting satisfaction targets based on these indices for managers at different levels. Staff input to designing or refining the questionnaires allows local research or planning activity and thereby assessment of issues on which management can take action. The CASPE approach offers a number of advantages: it is simple and flexible; it is cost-effective through using a computerised system linked to the existing patient administration system, and it can be incorporated as a routine part of the management process. This represents an improvement over previous methods which have been costly in the use of labour for data collection and have not been integrated with routine management information.

Evaluation of Outcomes

Meaning of Disability and Distress

Progress has been made in assessing outcomes at the individual level by focusing on dysfunction at a social and physical level as well as morbidity (and mortality). Despite the difficulties of defining and measuring 'good' or 'perfect' health, these approaches use individuals' subjective judgements about their quality of life to develop standard indicators that measure changes in medical, psychological and social functioning, i.e. in health status. The development of health indices of different types uses a similar basic approach: first, a taxonomy is set up of the states of health or capacities/functions or attitudes associated with good health, and second, individuals are asked to attach a value to each of these aspects using some kind of scoring system. In the case of establishing a single index a (subjective) weighting must also be given to individual elements. The identification of the scales and individual weightings are done by patients or clinicians or both. In all cases, of course, a general population must be identified against which to standardise the results. It is useful to look in detail at a UK example.

Rosser (Rosser and Kind, 1978) developed a set of descriptions of states of illness in two dimensions - disability and distress. There were eight levels of disability - from no disability or slight social disability, to being confined to bed and finally unconscious - and four levels of distress - from none to severe. These were combined to give 29 states of illness (an unconscious patient was assumed not to experience distress). Scores recorded by a sample of 70 including patients (psychiatric and medical), nurses (psychiatric and medical), doctors and healthy volunteers generated a valuation of each of the 29 states. It showed much steeper valuations, for example, for psychiatric patients and (their) nurses compared with medical patients and (their) nurses. There is a wide dispersion in scale valuations. The full table of results is set out below (Table 6.1),

Table 6.1

	Distress Rating			
Disability Rating	None	Mild	Moderate	Severe
1. No disability	1.0	0.995	0.99	0.97
2. Slight social disability	0.99	0.986	0.973	0.932
3. Severe social disability	0.98	0.972	0.956	0.912
4. Choice of work severely limited	0.964	0.956	0.942	0.87
5. Unable to undertake employment	0.946	0.935	0.9	0.7
6. Confined to chair	0.875	0.845	0.68	0.0
7. Confined to bed	0.677	0.564	0.0	-1.486
8. Unconscious	-1.028	-	-	-

1 = healthy, 0 = dead

based on further work by Rosser and others (Kind, Rosser and Williams, 1982). The results also suggest that some states, notably being confined to bed with severe distress, are valued as worse than death. The resulting scale is tentatively described as a ratio scale on the assumption that the principal objective of a health service is the relief of disability and distress; this implies a valuation of one for the state of no disability and no distress.

Quality Adjusted Life Years (QALYs)

Williams' (1985) important study on coronary artery bypass grafting sought to assess its effectiveness in terms of the effect on life expectancy adjusted for the quality of life. In this study three cardiologists were asked for judgements on the comparative profiles of health of various patients with angina who had, or had not, undergone coronary artery bypass grafting. They were asked to distinguish cases of severe, moderate and mild angina and express the profiles in terms of the Rosser disability/distress classification. This yields a table of cases with quality of life (QoL) values. The average life expectancy for each of case is discounted at 5% to allow for time preference. A total discounted QoL score is obtained for each of the alternatives of medical and surgical management and the difference between these is the theoretical quality adjusted life year (QALY) gain from surgical management. This figure is adjusted for the 30% of patients who have no symptomatic relief after surgery, and the loss of QALYs from the 3% perioperative deaths (compared with medical management). The discounted QALY gain for each procedure is then related to the present value of the additional cost of the procedure to give a present value of extra cost per QALY gained. The results give £5000 per QALY gained for heart transplant compared with £900 for valve replacement for aortic stenosis or £700 for pacemaker implantation for heart block.

This analysis was extended to cover other procedures suggesting that a pacemaker is more cost effective than treatment of end stage renal failure by haemodialysis (£11-14,000 per QALY gained) but less cost effective than hip replacement (£750 per QALY gained).

The evaluation of the QALY methodology introduces some difficult arguments. The first point is that it inevitably rests on a number of quality judgements, for example in deciding what aspects of health and quality of life should be included, what measurement techniques should be used, and whose preferences ought to be measured (e.g.the patients or their relatives?) (McGuire et al, 1988). Some sensitivity analysis of such valuations would be helpful. Second, it is argued that the data on mortality/morbidity on which QALYs are based are too inaccurate (Drummond, 1989). Third, it is also relevant that cost per QALY data are based on average values. Yet decisions in practice are about changes at the margin, and the costs incurred may vary with different levels of output for a particular intervention. Fourth, it is argued that broad comparisons across medical fields may be unwise and that such decisions must be taken politically: for example too rigorous an application of QALYs may have an adverse impact on particular groups of people.

But the figures do yield order of magnitude differences between costs of QALYs for different procedures and therefore should at least be considered. The crucial question in terms of the future of the methodology is whether it can yet form the basis of decision making, for example in planning and deciding between treatment priorities and planning, particularly if the conclusion on the basis of QALYs is counterintuitive. Raising the plausibility of QALYs to a level where they have a serious role in decision-making requires a great deal of technical work and a shift in attitude towards a greater emphasis on outcomes for health. The technical work would focus on improving the consensus over the use of quality of life measures and the basis on which this should be done. It may be that such a consensus is impossible to achieve so that the QALYs methodology would never be accepted in full by the professionals and the public.

Hospital Deaths

One interesting and direct study of UK hospital deaths was conducted by Paul Kind (1988). Unlike the US, where hospitals publish their mortality data, UK hospitals publish no outcome information. But data on one form of outcome can be extracted from the Hospital In-Patient Enquiry (HIPE) which is based on a sample of 10% of patients: these records contain information about discharge/death. Kind's study used these data for 1985 to look at the variation in mortality across regions: compared with a national average of 5.5%, the variation ranged from 4.5% in Oxford RHA to 5.9% in Mersey and East Anglia. Death rates were also calculated across specialty groups: general surgery ranged from 4.02% (Mersey) to 2.39% (Oxford); general medicine ranged from 12.61% (Mersey) to 9.42% (South Western); but death rates among patients diagnosed with mental disorders had a very wide range, from 1.24% in North West Thames to 12.75% in Mersey. Standardised mortality rates (SMR) for District Health Authorities range from 50% above to 50% below the national average of 5.5%. For example, if Grimsby's SMR were at the average national rate some 360 fewer deaths would be expected for this health authority.

However there are a number of limitations to these data so the conclusions of the study should be handled with care. HIPE data gives no indication of the severity of the disease so that, for example, where specialist hospitals take in a large number of complex cases, higher mortality figures would be expected and this should be corrected for (Charny, 1988). Another significant problem is that of defining the principal diagnosis and the fact that the HIPE data fails to identify patients with multiple diseases (or comorbidity) which would also lead to higher expected mortality. And HIPE data relate to admissions and not to individual patients so policies regarding the care of patients such as whether the terminally ill are treated at home or in hospital will distort mortality figures based on death rates per admission. Thus there may be very good reasons for variations in death rates based on case mix or the point at which patients contact the doctor, reasons which are hidden by the present data. The argument about whether such data should be published is therefore a fine one: the material shortcomings of the data may mislead, but publication at least allows questioning of the reasons for variations and provides an incentive to improve the data.

Perioperative Deaths

One of the most direct approaches to studying clinical outcomes in the UK was CEPOD (Confidential Enquiry into Perioperative Deaths). Over the calendar year 1986 all deaths occurring within 30 days of a surgical operation in three NHS Regions (Northern, North East Thames and Southern Western) were recorded and analysed: a total of 485,850 surgical operations were performed and 3,034 perioperative deaths recorded. Due to non-participation of a few (2.6%) surgeons or anaesthetists, 12.7% of these cases were lost. But the remainder revealed a number of shortcomings in anaesthetic/surgical practice (Buck, et al, 1987):

- mortality/morbidity conferences were the exception rather than the rule.

- lapses of delegation occurred with trainees undertaking work beyond their competence.

- examples were found of general surgeons undertaking non-urgent neurological surgery.

- in some instances patients who were moribund or terminally ill had operations which would not improve their condition.

- pre-operative assessment and resuscitation of patients were sometimes compromised by undue haste to operate.

There were marked differences between districts in the proportion of deaths considered to be avoidable. CEPOD demonstrates the feasibility and value of peer audit on a large scale.

The Newcastle Study on Short Term Clinical Outcomes

The study is based primarily on four specialties: general surgery (chole-cystectomy), medicine (diabetes), cardiology (angioplasty), and geriatrics. Initial work has also been undertaken in other procedures: knee replacements and rheumatology (rheumatoid arthritis). The approach is to build up a picture of patient outcomes expected by case type and over time, including the expected changes in patients' health status. Clinicians are involved in defining targets, and patients are assessed before the intervention, after the intervention and after three and twelve months. The methodology has four stages:

(i) Definition of patient reference group.

(ii) Identification of relevant indicators of clinical care and how these might change over time.

(iii) Identification of data required for indicators, the practicability of collection and its reliability.

(iv) Identification of targets and standards for each indicator and subsequent monitoring against these standards.

At present the most advanced specialties in the project (general surgery and general medicine) are at the stage of feeding back pilot data collected to clinicians for their views.

Marginal changes in patients' health will be traced over a year. This will include: clinical results measures, e.g. of angina or laboratory tests; adverse effects of treatment (if any) and presence or absence of any other specific symptoms, side effects or problems; and measures of function in terms of well-being or health status using the Nottingham Health Profile or the Sickness Impact Profile health assessment questionnaires.

This is a feasibility study. Clinical involvement is crucial; and key tests of success will be whether clinicians will choose to use the system after the pilot and whether it has any impact on practice. The study addresses both clinical and quality of life issues. On the clinical side the aim is to produce 'expected values' which represent a satisfactory outcome for the treatment. And on quality of life expected profiles for patients receiving different treatments immediately on discharge and after periods of three and twelve months will be developed.

Performance Measurement

Development and Definitions

Performance measurement is concerned with inputs, with intermediate outputs or throughputs, and with short term or immediate outputs. Thus it does not address long term outputs, much less outcomes. This section reviews aggregate performance measurement in the NHS - its history and current practice. The section concludes with a review of the latest set of National Health Service Performance Indicators (PIs) and a projection of their future usefulness.

The impetus for grand schemes of performance measurement has traditionally come from Central Government in the UK. This perspective implies a highly aggregative approach (at least at present) rather than one attuned to the needs of managers or practitioners within individual services. The initiative arose from the need to control public expenditure from the mid 1970s which led, under the Thatcher governments, to increasing questioning of what the public sector achieved. The history over the last decade has been one of increasing emphasis on the need for performance measurement, particularly in areas not previously addressed because of the difficulty of defining outputs. Examples include education and defence as well as health. The development of performance indicators has been driven by Central Government and been methodologically top-down; they have been part of the shift towards managerialism in the public sector and have generally been focussed on the needs of top-level managers or Central Government; they have been seen as shifting power from the periphery to the centre.

It is useful to distinguish between performance measures which quantify fairly precisely some aspect of interest such as productivity or an objective efficiency measure and performance indicators which are less accurate or address the relevant variable obliquely and may be suggestive rather than authoritative. For example, indicators may be used as tin-openers to indicate where performance merits more detailed sorting or exploration (Carter, 1989), rather than presenting a comprehensive view of activity.

Performance Measurement in the NHS

The NHS performance indicators do not measure performance as such
but can be used as a tool to ask questions and identify the means to
improve performance. The Department of Health has been working on
performance indicators (PIs) since 1981 and a set of about 145 were
published in 1983 as a result of collaborative work with the NHS. At the
same time IACC (Inter Authority Comparisons and Consultancy) at the
University of Birmingham produced a complementary package. Further
developments occurred in the Joint Group on Performance Indicators
which resulted in a new set of 425 PIs issued in 1985 using 1983/84 and
1984/85 data.

The 1985 PIs were organised into eight groups (acute services, children's services, the elderly, mental illness, mental handicap, support
services, estate management and manpower). They covered data on
finance, activity and manpower. The indicators were organised into a
hierarchy. First line indicators gave the relationship between activity (or
throughput) and input, e.g. hospitalisation rate by residents, or acute and
day cases compared with resident population; and second line indicators
gave the relationship between output and activity, e.g. percentage of
inpatient cases classified as immediate admissions. Another example
from obstetrics: first order, length of stay or delivery rooms for obstetric
bed; second order, percentage of admissions with no birth or number of
home births. Within this set of PIs only a handful of indicators relating
to outcome were included, e.g. neonatal mortality rates by weight.

A New Set of Performance Indicators

Developments in NHS performance indicators are continuing. The implementation from 1987 of the Korner recommendations on the collection
of a minimum data set for NHS management purposes means that a
uniform database for PIs will exist. A further Performance Indicators
Group was set up to address PI development and specifically to look at
how a new set of PIs can be based on Korner data.

A new set of indicators known as HSIs (health service indicators) was
published in 1989 covering all areas except community services for
1987/88. The data are based on Korner minimum data sets and are
organised into 42 family groups such as accident and emergency, hospital
beds or mortality; they include waiting lists and destination on discharge.
There may be around 2000 PIs at district level and developments will
include data on speciality costing (by seven major groups), data on

consultant episodes, and data on patients occupying beds. Hotel services will be included. There will be standardised information on expected values for length of stay, throughput and cost per case. The presentation of the new PIs will also be developed and will include two different approaches: a simple system which is easy to use with a mainly graphical output; and a more sophisticated spreadsheet system which allows direct access to data and can be updated with local data. The HSI data are presented at District level only and not at unit level. The Department of Health is also planning to release a set of district profile data items such as catchment population by specialty, socio-economic characteristics etc. This will allow districts to compare themselves with others with similar profiles.

Critique of PIs

A number of criticisms have been made about PIs, both in general and in relation to the NHS. Performance indicators have been described as public sector surrogates for information which would otherwise be made available through the market (Jackson, 1988). There is a wide range of expectations attached to PIs. One claim is that the objective of PIs must be to improve performance: to work effectively, indicators must show how to further the objectives of the organisation (Mullen, 1985). But for the NHS (and other sectors) objectives are not clear and the relationship between indicators and objectives is ambiguous. For example, a higher length of stay might better achieve the objective of prolonging life but would usually be taken as a sign of low efficiency (everything else being equal): thus the direction in which individual indicators point can be unclear. Similarly it is often not clear whether indicators are intended to be descriptive or prescriptive. Another major criticism is the risk that indicators as targets will distort priorities because managers and clinicians will aim to achieve them to the neglect of other priorities which cannot be so easily measured. All of this points to the need for a realistic idea of what PIs are for and what they can achieve.

A number of limitations have been identified affecting PIs in the NHS. They are too centralising and encourage detailed intervention by the DoH and Regions in Districts' work. There is a risk that Districts could be driven into meeting PI targets at the expense of innovation, quality and sensitivity to complementary services (Harley). There is a risk of improper use of PIs unless staff are experienced and understand their aims and limitations. One particular difficulty in the NHS is whether PIs 'belong to' managers or clinicians: surveys suggest that they are more used by managers at present but it is difficult to see how they can have full impact unless absorbed by clinicians, particularly as the package is increasingly refined towards the needs of districts and units.

A number of criticisms of the 1985 PIs were made in an evaluation of the use and validity of NHS PIs by CASPE (1987). This identified users of PIs as District General Managers, information specialists, district planners and Health Authority chairs with only specialists using the computer package directly. By contrast under half of Unit General Managers, finance officers and nursing advisers used PIs and very few Community Health Council secretaries. This pattern of use reflects the top down nature of existing 1985 PIs. CASPE found that PIs tend to be used reactively in response to issues and to a small extent in bids for resources. Limitations in PIs which restricted their use included:

- inaccuracies in data
- lack of relevance of PIs to unit/ward level
- lack of reliable comparators for particular district/units clustered on a case mix basis
- the two year lag in the data so the indicators are not timely
- lack of familiarity with PI packages within the NHS

PIs and no doubt Health Service Indicators (HSIs) will continue to be criticised for raising more questions than they answer, for being insufficiently tuned to local needs, and because they do not link into a population-based approach etc.

HSIs are mainly descriptive indicators rather than either prescriptive (i.e. related to measurable targets) or proscriptive (i.e. setting standards below which service should not fall) (Jackson, 1988). HSIs represent some advance in that they are seeking better to distinguish between different specialties. But they are clearly managerially-driven and restricted to data aggregated at District level. Arguably, more work should be put into developing flexible packages for use at intermediate levels of management such as the unit level. Nor is it clear whether proposals to facilitate comparisons across Districts by developing district profile items will be useful unless effort is also put into developing data in more usable forms such as producing templates of similar districts/units etc. as a means of defining the basis for comparison.

It is important to set the role of PIs in context. They were originally developed for management purposes to identify extreme levels of performance, and to trigger questions about process and to identify operational improvements - though this is subject to the criticism that performance measured via PIs is entirely relative and authorities may be encouraged to fall back to the average when they see themselves performing well. They should thus rather be seen as a contribution to the drive to look at performance locally and should be supplemented by local data and initiatives. One of the roles of the centre is to develop the methodologies and provide standardised data and expected outcomes so that local units have some norms against which to judge. Management should also identify clusters of similar units, districts or institutions as a basis for comparison. One real difficulty with PIs aimed at managers or clinicians is that they may be measuring activities which are beyond managerial control. The answer to this is clearly to construct PIs for flexibility: for example, rather than expressing PIs in terms of ratios where there is some redundancy due to repetition of denominators, absolute values could be given so that local managers can select ratios appropriate to their needs and capacities.

On the question of outcomes, both NHS PIs and other public sector performance indicators have made only limited progress in defining, let alone measuring, outcomes. Outcomes data within PIs have hitherto been limited to a handful of mortality measures. HSIs make some advance by including outcome related data on discharges (the destination of discharge of mental illness patients going outside the district or to local authority accommodation) mortality data (neonatal, children under 15, and standardised mortality rates) and perinatal mortality rate. But this is still very limited in scope.

Conclusions

In conclusion, it is worth considering briefly the implications of the changes proposed in the 1989 NHS White Paper, 'Working for Patients' (Cmnd 555) for assessment of process and outcomes and for the operation of performance indicators. The Government's plans involve a move towards greater competition in the NHS, towards a system which has been described as 'managed competition' (King's Fund Institute, 1989). This will involve extensive and explicit contracting for services between District Health Authorities or General Practitioners with their own budgets on the one hand, and existing District hospitals, other District services and the new self-governing trusts on the other. The emphasis in the White Paper on consumer satisfaction and medical audit suggests that the White Paper measures should help improve process quality. But it is important not to be too sanguine about this. A crucial aspect of contracting will be contracting for quality - finding ways of defining standards for services in contracts and ensuring that the standards stick. This is admittedly a difficult and innovative area but it is not clear that the Department of Health has yet got to grips with operationalising the issues involved.

The White Paper proposals have much less to offer on outcomes per se. There are no proposals which will specifically advance work on outcomes. There might nevertheless be some beneficial effects: for example, if medical audit is to be effective, specialists will increasingly need to define standards and protocols for treatment which will be linked to outcomes, and medical audit will perhaps focus more attention on outcomes such as death or health status. But progress in this area will continue to be gradual and piecemeal, probably building on work on QALYs and some of the work under way at CASPE.

Finally, the main effect of the White Paper on output and performance measurement will probably be to increase the demand for relevant and timely indicators. As the contracting process reaches down to unit level, unit management will increasingly demand indicators which are meaningful for them, such as data which allow comparison with other units with analogous profiles. The use of indicators will potentially therefore extend beyond senior management. And there will be increasing pressure to make indicators more outcome-related. But this expansion of HSIs will only happen if their accuracy is sufficient to command belief and if the development work on increasing their usefulness leads to a user-friendly output.

References

Buck, N., et al, (1987), *The Report of a Confidential Enquiry into Perioperative Deaths*, The Nuffield Provincial Hospital's Trust and the King's Fund, London.

CASPE, (1987), *Use and Validity of NHS Performance Indicators*, CASPE Research, 14 Palace Court, London W2 4HT.

Carter, N., (1989), 'Performance Indicators: Backseat Driving or Hands Off Control?', *Policy and Politics*, 17: 2.

Charny, M., (1988), 'Death Data: Do They Work?', *Health Services Journal*, 98 (5130), 1450-51.

Department of Health, (1989), *Working for Patients*, Cm 555, HMSO, London.

Devlin, H. B., (1988), 'Professional Audit; Quality Control Keeping up to Date.', *Balliere's Clinical Anaesthesiologys*, 2: 2.

Donabedian, A., (1988), *Exploration in Quality Assessment and Monitoring Volume I Definitions of Quality and Approaches to its Assessment*, Health Administration Press, Ann Arbor, Michigan.

Drummond, M.F., (1989), 'Output Measurement for Resource Allocation Decisions in Health Care', *Oxford Review of Economic Policy*, 5: 1.

Griffiths, R., (1983), *NHS Management Enquiry*, Department of Health and Social Security, London.

Gruer, R., et al, (1986), 'Audit of Surgical Audit', *The Lancet*, 4 January.

H.M. Treasury, (1989), *The Government's Expenditure Plans 1989-90 to 1990-91*, Chapter 14, CM 614, Department of Health, HMSO, London.

Jackson, P., (1989), 'The Management of Performance in the Public Sector', *Public Money and Management*, Winter .

Kind, P., Rosser, R., and Williams, A., (1982), 'Valuation of Quality of Life: Some Psychometric Evidence' in Jones-Lee, M.W., (ed.) *The Value of Life and Safety*, Elsevier/North Holland.

Kind, P., (1988), *Hospital Deaths - The Missing Link: Measuring Outcome in Hospital Activity Data*, Discussion Paper 44, Centre of Health Economics, University of York.

King's Fund Institute, (1989), *Managed Competitor*, Briefing Paper 9, King's Fund Institute, London.

McGuire, A., Henderson, J., and Mooney, G., (1988), *The Economics of Health Care*, RKP, London.

Mullen, P., (1985), 'Performance Indicators - Is Anything New?', *Hospitals and Health Services Review*, 81: 4.

Rosser, R., and Kind, P., (1978), 'A Scale of Valuations of States of Illness: Is There a Social Consensus?', *International Journal of Epidemiology*, 7: 4, 347-358.

WHO, (1988), *Priority Research for Health for All*, WHO Regional Office for Europe, Copenhagen.

Williams, A., (1985), 'Performance Indicators - Is Anything New?', *Hospitals and Health Services Review*, 81: 4.

Chapter 7

Performance Measurement and Review in Local Government*

David Henderson-Stewart

Introduction

The Audit Commission is responsible for the external audit of local authorities in England and Wales, and will shortly assume a similar responsibility for the national health service. It was established as an independent body in 1983, and at the same time the scope of its audit work was extended to include 'value for money' - helping local authorities to ensure that their services are provided economically, efficiently and effectively. It supervises the some 800 practising auditors - and up to half of their effort is devoted to value for money as opposed to traditional audit.

The Commission promotes the quality of auditors' work in various ways, notably by undertaking central studies of good practice. Their purpose is to help every local authority to learn from the best, and generally they concentrate on identifying and documenting good practice as it already exists, rather than undertaking basic research. The results of these studies are made available as public reports, and also in the form of more detailed guides for auditors. A key feature is usually a set of performance yardsticks that enable the auditor to gauge the scope for improvement at each authority and to set realistic targets for change.

These studies deal with specific areas of local authority work, for example, the care of children or the management of vehicles. However, the effectiveness of any council's service, and its ability to improve and to adapt to changing circumstances are also critically affected by its

---

* This chapter is based upon *Managing Services Effectively - Performance Review*, Management Paper No. 5, The Audit Commission, 1989.

overall management arrangements - for example its ability to draw up realistic plans, the way it manages its people, and its effectiveness in reviewing and controlling results. So a small part of the Commission's effort is also devoted to more general management topics. It is in the process of producing a series of short 'management papers' dealing with some of the key processes that are essential to the effective management of public services in general. The underlying theme is the need for councils' management processes to evolve in order to adapt to the more challenging and competitive environment now facing them. This chapter is drawn from a recent management paper, *Managing Services Effectively - Performance Review*.

Effective performance review has always been critical to the management of a local authority, or indeed any organisation, but never more so than today. There are several reasons for this. There is intense pressure for councils to be more accountable to the public, and a growing public concern about the quality of their services. Moreover, an increasing proportion of their work is now open to competition and contracting out; performance review is the key to managing any service subject to competition. At the same time, more and more authority is being delegated to front-line units such as schools. With less central control over 'inputs', or over the manner in which services are delivered, councils must now shift their emphasis to monitoring and reviewing the 'outputs' achieved.

There is universal agreement on the need for better performance review; the question is how to do it. Performance review is obviously harder in the public service than in the commercial sector. There are genuine difficulties in defining and measuring the 'output' of any public service, and much room for useful research in this area. Here, as elsewhere, the Audit Commission has not sought to advance the state of the art. Its objective is simply to outline what councils could do to improve their performance review, based on the current state of knowledge and employing techniques that are already in use. There are difficulties in implementing these techniques, but without seeking to minimise the underlying difficulties, the Commission also suggests that it is wrong to overstate the scale of the problem, or to use these difficulties as a reason for avoiding the explicit review of performance in areas such as education and social services.

Better performance review comprises two main tasks: better and more systematic assessment of the effectiveness and quality of services, and better-organised systems of monitoring and reporting performance. These form the subject of the following two sections of this chapter.

Measuring Performance

Performance review depends ultimately on defining what performance means, and then measuring it. The Audit Commission has found it useful to conceptualise the process as in Figure 7.1 which distinguishes costs, resources provided, outputs and outcomes. While outputs measure the use made of resources, outcomes reflect the ultimate value or benefit of a service to its users.

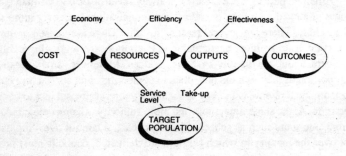

Figure 7.1

These measures provide the raw material for performance review. They normally only come to life in the form of performance indicators, based on the ratios between them, which can be monitored over time or compared with targets or with performance elsewhere. These are of three kinds:

- *Economy measures* show the cost of acquiring resources such as staff, premises or supplies.
- *Efficiency measures* show the outputs achieved in relation to the resource inputs, for example the cost per residential place.
  Where the service facility can be measured, it is also possible to measure its utilization, for example the occupancy of residential homes, or the utilisation of recreation facilities.

- *Effectiveness measures* show the final outcome of the service in relation to its output, for example the number of pupils passing an examination as a percentage of all the pupils in the age group.

It is important to define and measure the target population for each service. This provides the basis for two other performance indicators. The first measures level of service (for example, the number of places provided per elderly resident, or the number of leisure facilities in relation to the catchment population) while the second shows the take-up of services (for example, the proportion of the catchment population that use the swimming pool).

Once these performance indicators have been identified and measured, then the performance of the service can be monitored, and compared with the expected levels of achievement. Problems and opportunities can be spotted and investigated, and corrective action initiated where needed.

That is the theory of performance measurement. The practice is not always so easy. The most obvious difficulty is how to measure the 'outcome' or effectiveness of a service, given that it is usually easier to measure its 'output'. But output measures may be misleading or meaningless unless there is reasonable assurance about the effectiveness and quality of the service. The easiest things to measure are usually inputs. But this creates its own danger - the equivalent of Gresham's Law: the measurable drives out the un-measurable, and performance review is biased towards reducing or, indeed, increasing cost rather than improving effectiveness.

There is an extensive literature on the theory of performance measurement, which clearly underlines such difficulties, and emphasises the dangers of misleading performance indicators. While recognising the difficulties, the Audit Commission believes that it is wrong to conclude that performance measurement is quite so vulnerable, for two reasons. First, it is better to have incomplete or imperfect measures of performance than none at all. Simple indicators such as rent arrears, voids, or overdue repairs are partial and imperfect measures of the performance of a housing department, but this surely does nothing to detract from their usefulness to the managers and members concerned with this service. Second, many of the objections to simple measures of performance appear to assume that their audience has no judgement or common-sense. This assumption is simply incorrect. Most council members and officers who actually use performance measures are well aware of their limitations and pitfalls, and are perfectly capable of judging what conclusions can and cannot be drawn from them.

Performance indicators clearly can be interpreted without common sense, or willfully misinterpreted and exploited for adversarial purposes. For example there is a real danger that in the competition to attract pupils, some schools will quote misleading statistics, and some parents will be misled by them. But the solution is not to abandon the attempt to measure performance, or to censor the information, but rather to try to improve the measures, and to counteract the dangers of misinterpretation.

The Commission therefore believes that it is a disservice to local government to dwell too much on the theoretical difficulties of measuring performance. What is more useful is to propose practical ways in which local authorities actually can measure their performance, while avoiding the worst consequences of misleading indicators.

Measurement Issues

The cost of a service, and the resources it employs, is the one type of measure that should always be readily available, and is always important. It is wrong to place an exclusive emphasis on financial measures without regard for service standards or quality. But money is the ultimate scarce resource of every council, so any performance monitoring system must give a prominent place to costs.

This should be done by dividing all of the services of a council, and its back-up activities, into a series of distinct cost-centres, each with a budget that clearly identifies the costs that its manager is expected to control; and spending must be regularly and promptly measured against this budget. As money is spent in order to acquire resources such as staff, so a good financial control system should accompany financial figures (e.g. staff costs) with the underlying indicators that determine these costs, e.g. the numbers of staff actually in post, or the area of the premises on which costs such as heating and repairs are incurred.

The second level of measurement is the resources or service facilities that are actually provided, for example staff, premises, vehicles or energy, and the units of service that these collectively provide, for example the number of places in residential homes, or the number of library service points. Careful thought has to go into choosing the best way of measuring and comparing them.

Output means the service actually delivered to customers, for example the number of pupils educated by a school, the number of residents in an old peoples' home, or the number of admissions to a leisure centre. The main purpose of measuring outputs is to derive useful performance indicators, such as the utilisation of service facilities, or the take-up of a service in relation to its target population.

The main problem here is quality: poorly educated pupils simply do not represent the same output as those that are better educated. Leaving this aside, generally it is obvious what the outputs of a service are, and easy to measure them. However, it is worth thinking carefully about the best way of doing this. As discussed in Chapter 2 above, this depends upon the type of service involved. Possible examples are:

- **Response Time**. The key performance indicator for many council services is how promptly the service is provided - for example the average time taken to respond to fire calls, to determine planning applications, to relet councils houses, or to undertake repairs.

- **Tasks Completed**. Performance review should also be concerned with the actions being taken to improve services. It may be just as important to measure the completion of tasks such as the introduction of a new computer application.

- **Restricted Services**. There will never be enough places in old peoples' homes for all who might benefit from them. So almost the key indicator of performance is *who* uses them, to ensure that places are given to those that need them most. Likewise, a key issue in highways maintenance is directing the limited budget to those schemes that are assessed to be of highest priority.

The fourth dimension on which the performance of a service needs to be measured, or at least evaluated, is its 'outcome', or 'impact' - in other words its effectiveness in meeting users' needs or achieving its underlying purpose. This is, of course, the most fundamental aspect of performance that needs to be reviewed. The volume of resources devoted to education, and numbers of pupils educated have virtually no importance unless the desired educational impact is achieved.

As Table 7.1 shows for the case of secondary schools, some aspects of the outcome of education can be measured, for example examination results or the destination of leavers, while some cannot. Great care is needed in interpreting these measures, and they only deal with a part of outcome of the process of education. More generally, most other services simply have no outcomes that can practically be measured in quantitative terms. This is the main technical difficulty in reviewing performance, and unless there is some assurance about effectiveness, there is always room for doubts about the validity of such other performance indicators as unit costs. However, even if outcomes and effectiveness cannot be directly measured and counted, they can nearly always be evaluated in other ways. This is one of the main opportunities for improving performance review systems, and is discussed in the next section.

Table 7.1: Measuring Performance in a Secondary School

	QUANTIFIABLE	NOT READILY QUANTIFIABLE
RESOURCES	Costs Teachers, other staff Premises	
SERVICE PROVIDED	Teachers Curriculum (timetable)	Quality of teaching Content of curriculum
	Class sizes Support staff	Facilities Extra-curricular activities
	School places	
OUTPUT	Pupils, by age	Special needs Background factors
OUTCOME	Attendance Exam results	Behaviour Non-academic achievements
	Destination of leavers	

Evaluating Quality and Effectiveness

No matter what a service costs, or how generously it is provided, the most critical indicator of its performance is the value or benefit that it confers on its users. Simply measuring costs and quantities, with no regard for quality, is not a satisfactory basis for performance review. At the same time, once a council has some assurance about service quality, it can attach much more importance to other measures such as unit costs, making the whole performance review process more credible.

Those who practise or advocate performance review - notably the Audit Commission itself - are frequently attacked for insensitivity to quality or effectiveness. Whatever the strength of such criticisms, the solution should not be to abandon performance measurement, but rather to make sure that quality and effectiveness are given the attention that they deserve. This is undoubtedly the hardest issue, but it is far from insoluble. The simplest approach is to use proxy measures of impact, where these are available.

One of the reasons for providing recreation centres may be to occupy teenagers and so reduce vandalism. This impact may be hard to measure directly, but a fair test is simply to count the number of teenagers - or particular types of teenagers - that actually use the facilities. In a school, a rise or fall in the attendance rate may not matter greatly in itself, but it may be a useful proxy measure of part of the impact of the school on its pupils. A simple proxy measure for many services is the level of public complaints, or the level of customer demand and customer retention.

These are all imperfect measures of the real effectiveness of a service, and need to be used with caution; but they are a less expensive way of assessing effectiveness and quality. Where they are not available, and if outcomes and quality are crucial, there are two other main approaches: surveying customers' opinions, and professional quality control.

One alternative is evaluation by customers. In the commercial sector they are the ultimate arbiters of quality. If they have a choice between competing products, and if they pay the full cost, then their decision to buy (or not to buy) one particular product is normally a reliable indicator of its quality and value for money. And the private sector, unlike local government, makes extensive use of consumer surveys to provide more detail about the perceived quality of its products or services.

This is not quite so simple in the public services; many council services are effectively monopolies, where the customer has no real choice. Many are heavily subsidised or free, so it is not obvious that users would still be satisfied if they were charged the full cost. And some users are inherently likely to be poor judges - for example some of the clients of the social services (or of the police).

Nonetheless, customers can still be good judges of quality. The level of attendance at a recreation centre is not simply an indicator of its utilisation, but also of its quality. Popularity provides a reasonable guarantee that customers are benefiting from it. Poor use raises an immediate question about effectiveness.

This can be reinforced by simple surveys of users, recording their opinion of the current service, and their suggestions for what else might be provided. Surveys of tenants are clearly the best way of gauging the quality of public housing, and identifying the main opportunities for improvement. The same approach can also be used for some of the social services, especially those for the elderly.

Finally, the effectiveness or impact of most services can reasonably be gauged by inspecting and controlling the quality of the service itself in relation to accepted standards - by evaluating the process rather than the outcome. For example the purpose of providing street lighting, and the ultimate test of its quality or 'outcome', must include factors such as reducing crime and avoiding accidents - hypothetical outcomes that it is clearly impractical for a local authority to measure or evaluate on a regular basis. This is a task for research rather than for performance review. Research should question what form of street-lighting will achieve these objectives most effectively and at least cost, and should develop standards of good practice based on these findings.

Once such standards have been developed and promulgated, performance review can focus on the more modest and practical issue of whether the authority's street lighting actually meets accepted standards. If so, it is generally fair to assume that the service is providing the desired impact.

For many or most services, therefore, the review of quality and user satisfaction can be achieved by inspection and quality control over the service itself, and more particularly by an effective quality assurance system.

Quality Control

It is often claimed that performance review is easier in the private sector, because it has a simple and unambiguous 'bottom line', in terms of sales, prices and profit. By contrast, in the public service the key factor is quality, which is much harder to measure. There is only very limited truth in this contention. For most businesses, the quality of their products or services is just as critical to success it is in the public service, and just as difficult to define and measure. Well-managed companies attach the highest importance to quality, and to quality control. Indeed if there is one single characteristic of the most successful companies it is simply their total dedication to quality - Japanese industry provides the most obvious illustration, and there are a number of well-known examples within this country.

The same is true in local government: the best-managed councils, and the best managed departments, attach the highest importance to service quality. Many local authorities would learn a lesson from the systematic application of quality control found in the private sector and in the more general process of quality assurance.

Applying such methods to services such as education is not straight-forward, but there is the same need for a systematic approach. This will typically involve the setting of targets for quality, systematic inspection and control and regular reporting of results. These are simple rules, but in the Commission's experience they are seldom applied properly, even in education, which has the most extensive inspection function.

Quality Assurance

Quality control is intended to identify cases of poor service or poor quality, and to see that these are corrected. But the real goal is not simply correcting faults, but avoiding them. This can be promoted by an effective quality assurance process. Quality control forms part of this process, but the more important ingredient is that the provider of the service accepts the obligation not to deliver unacceptable quality. Quality assurance forms part of the contract between the supplier of a service and the client, as follows:

(a) The required quality standards are explicitly negotiated and speci-fied in the contract, and communicated to all involved, in particular to the suppliers' staff.

(b) The staff providing the service understand what quality is required, and are expected to maintain these standards in their own work. Thus employee training forms a major component of any quality assurance system. This is reinforced as necessary by the supplier's own internal quality audit.

(c) The supplier's quality control procedures are documented, and form part of the contract. There are officially approved bodies who specialise in the review and certification of suppliers' quality pro-cedures for this purpose.

(d) The client's assurance of quality rests primarily on the evaluation and testing of the supplier's own control procedures - what these specify, and how well they are actually applied.

(e) The client also exercises quality control over the service delivered. But this should operate as the 'long-stop'. Unacceptable service should not be delivered. If it is, this should trigger an intensive investigation of the suppliers' quality assurance procedures.

This relationship can be applied directly to any council service put out to contract, whether to a third party or to an in-house DSO. As well as specifying the standards to be provided, the contract should lay down the quality control procedures to be followed by the contractor. The client department's inspectors should then increasingly focus on monitoring the contractor's own performance in assuring quality.

Exactly the same principle can also be applied to other local authority services, treating the front-line service unit as the supplier, and the department itself as the client, acting on behalf of the council. This can be illustrated in three different types of activity: education, social services, and professional support services.

Running through all the current debate on education is a concern for improving quality. Statistical performance indicators can monitor certain facets of a school's performance; governors play a central role, as do parents; but these are no substitute for a well-organised system of professional quality assurance.

In line with the quality assurance model, this needs to be based on the foundations of a clear agreement between the LEA and the school about the basis on which the school will be judged; teachers who understand what is expected of them, and have the professional qualifications (and the in-service training) to deliver it; front-line quality control exercised by senior staff within the school and a well-organised professional inspectorate.

Education is the one local authority service with an established inspection function. It is the Commission's view that inspectors' work will need to be more systematic in future, with a clearer division between inspection and advice, more explicit monitoring of schools' internal appraisal methods, and of the quality of their teaching, and clearer recording and reporting of their findings.

Although social service departments inspect private facilities, there is not the same tradition of internal inspection. Yet it is hard to see why not. Few other services can have such a critical impact on their customers, or customers who are so badly placed to choose for themselves or to complain. The need for quality assurance is just as great as in education, if not greater.

Finally, much important work is performed by 'professional' staff, such as architects, surveyors, lawyers and accountants. It goes without saying that the quality of their work is critical, and councils clearly need some assurance that this is maintained at the highest level. The professions themselves provide some elements of a quality assurance function. They guarantee appropriate qualifications and promote standards of probity and work. And local authority professionals, unlike some others, are directly supervised by other members of their profession.

Despite this, the Audit Commission suggests that local authorities, and the senior managers of such professional staff, should consider whether there is a case for a more explicit quality audit approach. This might be on the lines of the system of peer-group evaluation that is now being developed in the medical profession, and is outlined in the recent set of White Papers on the reform of the National Health Service. And as the cost of in-house services is increasingly being challenged, for example by using 'practice accounts', so it is only fair to apply equally stringent tests of quality to private-sector services.

Monitoring and Reporting Performance

The purpose of measuring performance is to compare actual results with targets or yardsticks, and so to identify potential problems, and decide when corrective action is needed. Developing an effective monitoring and reporting system comprises four main steps:

(a) identify the key issues for each service, and the key processes that genuinely need to be monitored; and select the performance indicators that measure them;

(b) clarify responsibilities for monitoring performance - who needs to monitor what, and how often, including members, senior management, and the front-line managers of each service;

(c) set targets or yardsticks, including quality objectives, that indicate whether performance is good or bad, or at least getting better or worse.

(d) design and produce the appropriate reports.

Identifying Key Performance Indicators

Some services readily generate large volumes of performance statistics; others are harder going. However, monitoring performance is not simply a matter of scanning whatever statistics happen to come to hand. For each service, the task is to decide what are the key issues and the key aspects of performance that genuinely need to be monitored, and then to focus on the performance indicators that relate to them.

Deciding which performance indicators are sufficiently important to need regular monitoring is a matter of judgement, and depends to some extent upon the audience, the time-period, and local circumstances. Some issues are critical within, or receive higher priority from, some councils than others.

In choosing the critical indicators, it is often useful to make a distinction between operational performance, that needs to be monitored at regular intervals, and underlying performance (for example quality and effectiveness), that may be just as critical, but which it would not be sensible to debate every month, even if the information were available.

Identifying the critical indicators of performance calls for selectivity - leaving aside or summarising details in some areas, making a deliberate effort to obtain more data in others, and sometimes accepting that it is not worth the cost of collecting all the information that would ideally be useful.

Clarifying Responsibilities

Councils' organisations form distinct pyramids. Front line managers report to service heads or area supervisors who report to chief officers - often with one or two intervening layers; and chief officers report to their committee and to the chief executive. All managers in the chain need to review the performance of the activities for which they are responsible. That requires an organisation structure which assigns clear responsibilities, and then a system to provide each manager with the information that they need.

At the top of the pyramid are the members. Members cannot possibly monitor every aspect of every service at every meeting, nor should they. So monitoring is an activity that needs to be delegated, like management. Members can fulfil their responsibility by means of a delegated monitoring scheme under which they regularly monitor a limited set of measures that they judge to be most critical, with an annual review of the whole service; they ensure that officers are adequately monitoring everything else, at the appropriate detail and frequency; they require any deviations beyond a certain level of significance to be reported to them immediately.

The same principle should extend down the line from chief officers to front-line managers. Every manager should monitor the activities he or she controls directly, and, in less detail, those controlled by their subordinate managers. Reports to managers at lower levels will generally cover a narrower range of activities than those to higher levels, but they need to contain more detail, and to be more frequent. Different management levels tend to make different kinds of decisions: front-line managers focus on immediate action, while senior management is more concerned to spot and investigate possible problems, and to review underlying performance. Front-line reports should therefore contain more raw information, e.g. the actual number of arrears cases and their value, while those at a higher level should more often be expressed as performance indicators, e.g. arrears as a percentage of the amount collectable.

A weakness in most councils' performance monitoring systems is the lack of systematic information to front line managers, and about front line performance. For example LEAs are awash with information about their schools, yet this is mainly used for LEA-wide monitoring or simply for inclusion in statistical reports. Few LEAs use this information to produce useful monitoring reports about individual schools, to help governors, head-teachers, and LEA staff to monitor and compare their performance. The opening page of such a report is illustrated in Table 7.2.

Table 7.2: Statistical Profile for a High School - Page 1

		1987/8	1988/9		
PUPILS ON ROLL	12-	112	104		
	13	115	109		
	14	127	111		
	15	141	126		
	16+	1	1		
	Total	496	441		
Standard Admission Number		160	160		
Maximum Accommodation		680	680		cf City
Occupancy Rate		73%	65%		79%
% attendance (12-16)		87%	91%		91%

				Averages	
		1987/8	1988/9	City	National
STAFFING (Sept 1988)					
Teaching Staff (fte)		27.3	23.7		
Pupil-Teacher Ratio		18.2	16.8	19.3	18.7
Teacher Contact Ratio		71%	69%	75%	76%
Support Staff (fte)		5.7	5.4		
CLASS SIZES (Sept 1988)					
Av Group	2nd year	25.1	23.7	24.8	24.7
Sizes	3rd year	22.3	21.9	22.5	22.0
	4th year	20.4	20.0	19.9	20.4
	5th year	18.0	17.1	18.1	18.0
% Classes	<15 pupils	15%	18%	14%	15%
by size	>30	4%	0%	15%	10%

Subsequent pages would cover the curriculum offerred; national assessment results; GCSE results; destination of leavers; and expenditure compared to budget and to average costs per pupil.

Finally, councils have an obligation to report to the public. Traditionally this has focused on their responsibility to rate-payers. Most councils now publish broader annual reports than this; and an increasing number provide very extensive detail about their activities. Councils are also under pressure to report directly to the users of their services. Schools have to make a wide range of information available to the public; and the government has just announced that every housing authority will be required to publish some basic performance indicators of interest to their tenants. Service users will normally be most interested in indicators of the service provided, and of its effectiveness. However, in the special case of housing, tenants themselves bear the council's costs, and so should be equally interested in measures of economy and efficiency.

Setting Targets or Yardsticks

There is little point reporting performance indicators without some kind of target or yardstick that indicates whether the figures are good or bad, or better or worse than expected. As a general rule, any performance indicator that a council monitors should have some kind of comparative figure set beside it. There are two possible approaches: setting targets, or using comparisons such as last year's figures or averages for other authorities.

Management theory states that every activity should have explicit targets set for it, and performance should be measured against these targets. This is the way every council controls its spending - the budget being the target - and the way most control their manpower, setting establishment targets for each section of the organisation. Practice varies widely for other types of performance: some councils draw up plans or targets for almost every indicator that they monitor, others do not.

It is important to avoid theoretical or arbitrary targets, and the danger of internally-set targets is that they are liable to be subjective, especially if they are set by those providing the service. There are three other more objective comparisons. The simplest is simply a comparison with last year. This may be the best or the only relevant yardstick that is available. It may be hard to gauge what a swimming pool's admissions or a school's examination results ought to be, but it is always interesting to know whether these are improving or getting worse. As a general rule, monitoring reports should always include last year's figure, or several years' figures, as a guide to assessing longer-term trends.

The natural comparison for front-line activities such as schools, social work districts or local housing offices is the average performance of similar units. The information is readily available; it refers to the same period, and does not suffer from the problems of definition that often make it difficult to relate to national figures. Such comparisons become increasingly useful as operations are decentralised.

For units such as schools the standard monitoring report should probably include both last year's results, and the average results of all other comparable schools. Table 7.2 above illustrates how such comparisons could be used in reporting some of the performance indicators for a school.

Finally, where there are no in-house comparisons for a service as a whole, or for any activities that do not split into separate units, the best yardstick may be national averages or benchmarks. Plenty of information and comparative statistics are available, for example CIPFA statistics, and the Audit Commission's Profiles; guidelines and standards put out by central government and other national bodies; and the good practice indicators developed as part of the Commission's special study work.

A large number of benchmarks figures are set out in the Data Supplement to the Audit Commission's *Performance Review in Local Government* series. Subsequent issues of the volume will revise some of its good practice guidelines, and expand its content to include concrete illustrations from individual authorities.

Production of Reports

The last stage in the process is to design and produce the required reports. Decisions about what information and comparative indicators to include in any monitoring reports depend upon the people for whom the report is intended, the decisions they have to take and the frequency of these decisions. The report should contain the minimum information needed to satisfy these requirements.

The exclusion of less critical items from regular reports does not mean that they are not monitored or reported. Members or senior managers should expect that any exceptional problems in any areas should be promptly reported to them, for example problems in a children's' home, or a sudden increase in bad debts. They should be dealt with on the exceptions reporting principle. Indeed, top-level monitoring reports might usefully contain an open page reserved for this purpose, which would also be the place to report the completion of key tasks.

Like any kind of communication, monitoring information is more effective if it is well presented. Much the most important aspect of good presentation is simply economy or brevity. A good report is one that contains the minimum number of figures necessary to convey the required information. Every extra statistic added to a report tends to detract from the clarity and impact of the rest. Brevity means both eliminating statistics of marginal value, and devising the most economical means of displaying the indicators that do need to be included.

Many authorities have now enabled their managers to access information directly on local terminals, and to print off their own reports. This has great advantages in convenience and cost. But there is still value in sending managers periodical monitoring reports on paper - brief, attractively laid out, and printed to a high standard - the purpose being to ensure that the manager receives a properly presented report.

Monitoring Quality

Finally, reporting and monitoring should not solely be concerned with the indicators of performance that can be quantified. Assessments of quality and effectiveness do not usually need to be monitored every month or every quarter. However they must have a regular place on the agenda of members and senior management. One approach is for members to hold an annual meeting of each committee mainly devoted to performance review. At this meeting, the question should simply be asked of every service: what assurance do we have of its quality and effectiveness? The available information, e.g. from user surveys, or from professional inspection and quality control would be summarised; and where there are gaps these would be all the more obvious.

Conclusions

There is universal agreement about the need for better performance review in local government, and most of the suggestions made in this chapter present few practical difficulties. Why then is progress often so slow? What else is needed?

The Audit Commission's experience suggests that the other essential ingredient is simply the proper level of commitment. Genuine performance review is not always a comfortable process; it means appraising performance objectively, admitting to weaknesses or failures, grasping nettles, and taking action. This is often difficult, especially in the open environment of local government; and it is all too easy to introduce a performance review system that goes through the motions without genuinely achieving its purpose.

This commitment is needed at every level of a council's organisation: departments, central management and members. Services are delivered by departments, generally staffed and managed by professional officers, with a high degree of commitment to their service. Effective performance review may require a distinct change in management style, in which senior management monitors and reviews the quality of their services on a more objective basis. They should retain all their commitment to the objectives of the service, but not necessarily to the way in which it is currently being delivered. This change happens automatically whenever a service is contracted out. However the client-contractor model needs to some extent to be adopted even in departments whose front-line units remain part of the organisation.

At the level of central management a difficulty arises from the fact that many councils effectively form a rather loose federation of committees and linked departments. Compared to the private sector, their constitution usually gives rather strong powers to the treasurer, and rather weak formal authority to the chief executive. Hence the generally tight control over financial matters, and the less systematic and searching review of performance in a wider sense. Effective performance review across a council as a whole almost certainly requires a strong chief executive, with clear responsibility for the process, and with adequate quality for this purpose.

Finally, members play different roles at different authorities. However they are always ultimately responsible for the activities of their council, and performance review must be one of their main responsibilities. At a company board meeting, the review of the previous period's results is normally the core item on the agenda, and the first item for discussion. Yet Council and Committee agendas commonly include no reference at all to current performance.

Members must also be committed to the process. The Audit Commission believes that members in many local authorities are too closely involved with the day to day running of their services, too closely identified with the status quo and sometimes too ready to defend bad performance, to the prejudice of their real responsibilities towards their customers and rate-payers.

Chapter 8

Performance Indicators and the Management of Professionals in Local Government

David Burningham

Introduction

The problems which sometimes arise between general managers and professionals are common to many organisations, but in local government this relationship is particularly difficult for the following reasons:

(a) the organisation of departments into specialist groups such as planners, lawyers and social workers. This often reflects the way services are delivered and creates strong feelings of identification with the department;

(b) professional and departmental loyalties are further reinforced by the close relationship between service Committee Chairmen and their Chief Officers (COs). The accountability of COs to the Council is frequently channelled through Committee Chairmen rather than through the Chief Executive which makes corporate management difficult and weakens the role of an executive coordinator;

(c) although in the last 15 years the appointment of strong Chief Executives backed by corporate managers has helped to reduce these problems, difficulties remain; general managers are regarded with suspicion by many professionals; as one Chief Executive has observed, 'management' is sometimes 'almost a term of abuse - a function of less worth than being a real professional' (Bichard, 1989).

In principle, the use of performance indicators ought to reduce the tension between general managers and professionals. The establishment of agreed criteria and a system of measures against which performance be judged should reduce the need for what many professionals regard as 'niggling' *ad hoc* enquiries by general management. PIs should facilitate management by exception and promote a strategy of 'hands-off rather than hands-on' control (Carter, 1989).

In practice, PIs may sometimes actually widen the gap between professionals and general managers. The reasons can be seen by comparing the operating ratios used by managers in the private sector with the three Es (economy, efficiency and effectiveness) of the public sector (Figure 8.1).

In both environments, ratios are used for comparing organisations. The Audit Commission Profiles were designed with just this purpose in mind, along the lines of private sector inter-firm comparisons. The family of private sector ratios is linked by the 'bottom line' of profitability and sales. This gives at every point a potential indication of comparative strengths or weaknesses in key areas of sales and production. Despite superficial similarity, there is no such link running through the triad of ratios that comprise the three Es in the public sector. Because there is no agreed way of valuing disparate outputs which are not marketed, the crucial Effectiveness ratio - the basis for the bottom line - is ambiguous.

What is the influence of PIs on the management of public sector professionals? Pollitt (1986) has argued that the managerial model 'with its emphasis on costs and quantifiable ratios can squeeze out consideration of what sort of performance we are really interested in'. It can illustrate what Williams (1985) has called the 'relationship between the low-level indicators of performance and the high-level objectives of the system'. The consequence of this, in some instances, has been to polarise general managers and professionals. Some PI systems have tended to place professionals, who might be regarded as custodians of issues relating to Effectiveness - the quality of service delivery and technical performance - in opposition to measurement centred on economy and efficiency.

This is not to imply that professionals are not concerned with resource management or that they give lower priority to questions of economy or efficiency. Many of them, especially within their specialist departments, are line managers. It is simply that the fragmented nature of the public sector PIs contributes to antipathy and tensions without means of resolution. As a substantial literature shows, the special position of professionals within organisations is not exclusively a problem of the public sector (Blau and Scott, 1963; Caplow, 1964; Hughes, 1981; Lupton, 1983). Nevertheless, PIs in the market sector, unlike those in the public sector, do provide measures of the trade-off between quality and costs and the

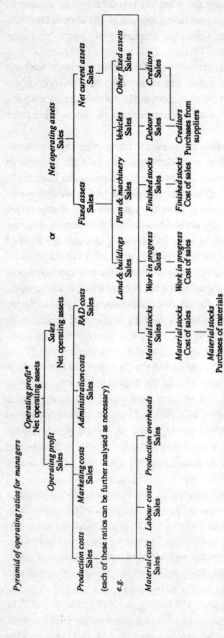

Figure 8.1: Private Sector Ratios

impact of each on sales and profits. While this in itself does not remove the tensions associated with professional groups, it does provide a rational basis for argument and negotiation. For example, arguments about the value of a high quality R and D programme or improved customer service through a stronger dealer network can be assessed with reference to the effects in the long and short run on profit margins and turnover. In the public sector, in the absence of a bottom line which links indicators, contentious issues between the various stake holders - clients and pressure groups, general managers and professional providers - are less easily resolved and may require a political process for their solution.

One response to this problem has been the search for better indicators and their incorporation in systems of performance review. Chapter 7 above by David Henderson-Stewart contains some useful practical suggestions for doing this. However, this chapter, based on case studies of local authority experience with PIs and other material, argues that the solution to the problems of performance measures is not exclusively one of finding better indicators. It is also one of finding better ways of integrating PIs with the working practices of the organisation to which they are applied. Otherwise, there is a danger that if PIs are produced in isolation and bolted on to an organisation, they acquire a momentum of their own with unintended consequences.

The Case Study

The literature on PIs is long on pathology and short on prescription. It is said that what is needed is not further diagnosis of inadequacies but better PIs. The justification for offering the following case study, which illustrates many of the deficiencies of indicators, is that it helps to identify a general framework, within which PIs can be more fruitfully applied.

This is an account of the use of performance measurement over a four year period in a local authority Planning Department. The material presented here was gathered in the course of a Brunel consultancy/research project. To maintain confidentiality and avoid identification from Audit Commission Profiles, the data have been altered or presented in index form. Nevertheless, the trends shown here reflect actual events.

Although the account concerns only one department, it has wider relevance because it has a number of features shared by other local government departments attempting to introduce PIs:

(a) a significant proportion of professional staff accustomed to a substantial amount of discretion in the way they planned and organised their work;

(b) the use of PIs to overcome specific problems - bottlenecks, blurred accountability;

(c) the provision of data for individual performance appraisal in connection with performance related pay.

The Planning Department, under the management of a Director and Deputy, was organised into two divisions: Forward Planning and Development Control:

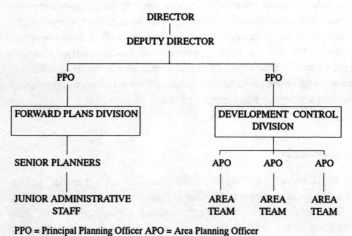

PPO = Principal Planning Officer APO = Area Planning Officer

Figure 8.2: Planning Department

The Forward Planning Division prepared and updated a plan for the whole area, applying the strategy of the Council and providing a framework for the preparation of district and action area plans. The Development Control Division's principal tasks were: dealing with planning applications; development of district plans; initiating and encouraging small scale developments - reclamation and improvements. The Development Control Division was divided into three teams, each under an Area Planning Officer responsible for activities in a particular area. The rationale behind this structure was that each team would get to know a particular area and its people thoroughly, improving the consistency and speed with which planning applications were processed. It was also hoped that this would facilitate the development of realistic district plans and initiatives, with public involvement.

The principal problems facing the Planning Department, which had provoked critical comment from elected members and the local press, were seen to be: the need to deal more quickly with a high level of planning applications, which were being processed at a rate of five staff days per application - lower than the average for comparable local authorities; and the need to revise and improve local plans upon which progress had been rather slow.

Output measurement eventually covered what were regarded as the principal outputs of the Department - the production of local/district plans; advice to the council and other departments in the form of reports and surveys; planning applications determined. Performance indicators for these activities are summarised below:

Table 8.1: Planning Department

Measures of Performance	Year 1	Year 2	Year 3	Year 4
Adherence to local/district plan programme:				
Actual as % of annual target	56	60	85	95
Advice to Council and Other Departments:				
Major reports/surveys	44	50	57	64
Public consultation meetings (index)	100	90	111	120
Planning applications determined	2000	2400	2600	2900
Index of total departmental costs (Year 1 prices)	100	107	109	111

From these results it would appear that the introduction of performance measurement was completely vindicated. With changes in organisation the labour cost per planning application fell by 27 per cent, 20 per cent of which was due to increase in productivity and seven per cent to more extensive use of junior administrative staff to process the simpler applications. Redeployment of staff and reorganisation in the Forward Plans Division contributed to similar changes in its performance indicators.

However, the scheme did not measure all aspects of the work of this Department. It did not, for example, reflect the work of consultation between and within Divisions. Nor did it measure work on consultation with individual members of the public and time spent at public participation meetings, although the number of meetings was included in the index of output. As the following table indicates, less time was spent on each of these activities.

Table 8.2

% of Time spent On	Year 1	Year 2	Year 3	Year 4
Inter-divisional meetings	10	8	7	4
Intra-divisional meetings	9	9	8	6
Public consultation/ participation	15	12	7	8

The flow of informal communications was reduced because contributions to inter- and intra-divisional meetings did not count in the measurement scheme. Only formal written documents were included in output measurement. There was an attempt to incorporate inter-divisional advice in reports, but this proved too cumbersome and was abandoned. Although it could be argued that the fall in meeting time was the result of the new management style - meetings were more efficient - it was evident that the content of inter-divisional communications was reduced. The Area Planning Officers, for example, were not getting full advice from Forward Planning on sampling and questionnaire design to help in assessing public opinion in the localities. Conversely, Forward Planning was less well informed from Development Control about what was happening in each area.

It was the intention of this particular Planning Department not to be an administrative machine but to encourage consultation through contacts between the Development Control Division and local people. The output measurement scheme contributed to a contrary effect. The emphasis on the achievement of targets for processing planning applications reduced time spent on public consultation by nearly 50 per cent. Although the number of meetings recorded in output measures did not appear to have declined, the quality of these meetings fell. Growing disquiet among residents about environmental issues, intensified by the lack of consultation, was reflected in an increasing volume of protest to members and letters to the local press, as well as opinion surveys:

Table 8.3: Residents' Opinion Survey

What do you think of the emphasis the Council places on the environment?

	Too Much (%)	Right Amount (%)	Too Little (%)	Don't Know (%)
Year 1	2	58	27	13
Year 4	2	46	43	9

One source of difficulty arose because the performance measurement scheme took little account of the nature of planning work and the way in which the professionals in the Department organised themselves, which was quite different from the formal hierarchy of the organisation chart. From the researchers' observation, communication between different planning groups was not passed up within each group but tended to be lateral, often without involving the Principal Planning Officers in any way. The content of communications in the Department was often quite informal, consisting of exchanges of information and advice rather than instructions and decisions.

Because the demands on the Department exceeded its capacity, priorities had to be decided and work programmed. Underlying the relaxed style of working was a more formal process of assigning and assessing work by senior officers and their subordinates. Undoubtedly the introduction of performance measurement strengthened this. Nevertheless, a balance needed to be struck between the advantages of flexibility arising from the informal style of management and the more formal structure necessary for planning and control. The adopted PI scheme tipped the balance towards the latter. For example, in the Development Control Division it was usual for Area Team members to spend time in informal discussions on planning applications - pooling of experience and collaborative work which provided useful guidelines for staff and ensured consistency in dealing with applications. The impact of performance measurement reduced time spent on meetings of this kind within the Department by a third. The effect of this was not reflected in the output measures, since they did not include quality, which in this context means permitting development consistent with the plan in a way that reflects the objectives of the Council.

Performance measurement sometimes restricted, in a counter-productive way, discretion shown in the organisation of other aspects of departmental work. Prior to the introduction of PIs, it had been customary to allocate some of the more complex planning applications to junior staff, so that they could gain experience under supervision. With the introduction of performance measurement linked to performance-related pay, this training process was neglected in an effort to raise productivity and associated merit increments. As with qualitative aspects of the work, it was difficult to measure training in a satisfactory way.

At the core of these issues lay unresolved differences between alternative systems of evaluating performance. There was the 'professional' or peer review system of assessment by planning officers, which was in place before the comprehensive scheme of PIs was introduced. It formed the basis for individual performance appraisal and career development. Comment on Plans was also invited from planners and planning consultants of distinction outside the Department. Alongside this was an entirely numerical system of PIs, which could be called 'managerial' in the sense that it could be interpreted by general managers and the Performance Review Committee without much recourse to the judgement of planning officers. Although it was intended that the two modes of assessment should complement each other, it was the managerial PI system which became dominant. It also figured largely in determining performance-related pay. All this created some resistance to PIs and some resentment among planners in the Department who felt that their professional judgement was in some way being devalued.

Conclusions from the Case Study

(1) The use of performance indicators can improve organisation and raise productivity.

(2) Output measurement may, however, have unintended effects on the organisation to which it is applied. Specifically it can affect:

  (a) the exercise of individual initiative and discretion in the use of resources;

  (b) the pattern of working relationships between groups and individuals;

  (c) responsiveness of an organisation to demands made on it.

(3) The inclusion of outputs which satisfy the criteria of being consistent and easily measured may lead to a neglect of other activities or qualities that do not meet these criteria.

Problems identified in the course of this case study, which are consistent with experience elsewhere, are not the result of inadequacies of PIs. Indeed, the PIs chosen had many of the qualities which Cave et al (1988) and others would include on a check list of desirable features. It is not only a question of the soundness of PIs but also of the way in which they are used. Even rather sketchy indicators, handled with care and properly integrated with the organisation in which they are used, can be effective. What this case study and other experience point to is the need for some way of putting PIs in context - ensuring that they are grafted rather than bolted on to organisations. Not every aspect of performance measurement need necessarily become a battle ground for between general managers and specialist professionals. The prospects for successfully implanting PIs in an organisation can be seen with reference to the purposes for which they can be used. Although the applications are varied, they fall into three distinct but connected groups (Knight 1989):

(a) *Accountability* - PIs as an expression of the key areas of performance for which the organisation, unit or individual is being held accountable by those on whose behalf the work is being done.

(b) *Control* - PIs used by managers to get early warning if performance starts to fall below the expected level or norm, so that corrective action can be taken - not to be confused with the more public PIs used to monitor accountability.

(c) *Development* - PIs as part of a learning cycle in a process of intervention and change management, intended to improve performance.

It is when these distinctive elements are not fully considered that assessment schemes may be introduced in a way that provokes considerable suspicion among line managers and professionals. No single system of indicators can satisfy the whole range of objectives. For example, PIs for control purposes need to be more selective and computed more quickly than those for public accountability.

Whereas PIs for public accountability are external to a department or organisation, the control and development functions are internal and should be chosen by the users - those directly in charge as well as client groups - not by people outside the system. It is here that the sense of ownership and commitment to PIs can be strong among professionals and managers. Unfortunately, external accountability is usually the starting point for the introduction of PIs, often - as was seen in our case study - in response to the imperative of an acute problem, leaving little scope for negotiation. Consequently, defensive attitudes and hostility extend to all aspects of performance measurement. PIs are seen as emphasising what Argyris (1962) has described as 'direction, control, rewards and penalties' which may tend to decrease openness, the capacity to experiment and willingness to take risks.

This view is further reinforced when the setting of targets for introducing performance measurement appears to carry with it the implication that failure to keep to schedule is in itself an indicator of poor performance. In the Departments we observed, there was something of a competitive element in the introduction of performance measurement, with the pressure on Departments to produce indicators as quickly as possible. If any department dared to suggest that it needed fewer indicators on the grounds that they were not particularly useful, it might have been seen as something of a laggard with inefficiency to hide.

Professionals and line managers within professional departments may not choose to initiate PIs for any of the reasons given. But if they find themselves in the position of being pressed to adopt PIs by external agencies, it makes sense to persuade them to use the situation as an opportunity to improve their own effectiveness. A number of practical steps which are often overlooked can be undertaken to secure the involvement and support of professionals for measurement schemes.

Firstly, a policy document can be compiled setting out a strategy for performance indicators. This would include:

(a) a statement in operational terms of what it is intended to achieve;

(b) an indicative timetable (both this and (i) above will help to eliminate the competitive scramble to see who can introduce the most indicators);

(c) guidance on the criteria for the selection and use of indicators;

(d) criteria and mechanisms for the evaluation and improvement of performance measurement schemes;

Secondly, it is helpful to have a Steering Group to assist in the task of preparing the policy document and monitoring the subsequent developments. Its membership should comprise representatives of the departments and units using the scheme, together with relevant external agencies (including clients) and a member of the Corporate Management Group, or whoever is responsible for coordination. It can provide a forum for evaluating experiences with PIs and establishing best practice. It also provides a point at which the dialogue and negotiation about indicators, and hence the sense of ownership so often lacking, can take place.

Thirdly, a realistic estimate is required for the resources needed to meet the aim specified in the policy document. If these are not available then a less ambitious series of targets will need to be set. Alternatively, instead of all departments being expected to advance simultaneously with indicators, it might be feasible to concentrate on a few improvements of indicators which are most likely to yield results. Thought also needs to be given to the question of resources for measuring effectiveness, particularly survey sampling methods for testing user opinion.

Implementing PIs

It would clearly be naive to assert that, by following the steps outlined here, the path for the introduction of PIs is a smooth one. Some of the difficulties can be resolved by participation and consultation. Others are a matter of conflict of interest between the parties involved, to be settled by bargaining or coercion within the power structure. Nevertheless, our observations suggest that the counter-productive aspects of performance measurement can be minimised by identifying those areas where participation will be fruitful and those issues which are potential points of conflict. This accords with experience elsewhere, for example the well documented case study of performance evaluation for managers in New York City which foundered because of poor implementation (Fletcher, 1985).

It is apparent from this and other studies that the positive or negative attitudes of professionals and other managers to PIs depend upon the way in which the measurement scheme is specified and introduced. This is not a cosmetic exercise of presentation, rather the emphasis is placed on various reasons for adopting PIs with the opportunity for the professionals to participate in formative stages. This is best achieved within a framework involving the sequence shown in Figure 8.3: *Analysis → Specification → Integration → Evaluation*

The desirable characteristics of PIs can be grouped under the six headings: (1) Relevance, (2) Congruence, (3) Ambiguity, (4) Cost, (5) Cheatproofness, (6) Aggregation. Although there is some general agreement about this list, in practice it is unlikely that any indicator will possess all the features listed. A PI might score highly on one characteristic at the expense of another. For example, the disaggregation of data necessary to monitor performance at unit or even individual level might substantially raise the costs of collection. Similarly, indicators which are highly relevant are sometimes complex and difficult to interpret, whereas unambiguous PIs may give a partial or simplified reading of events.

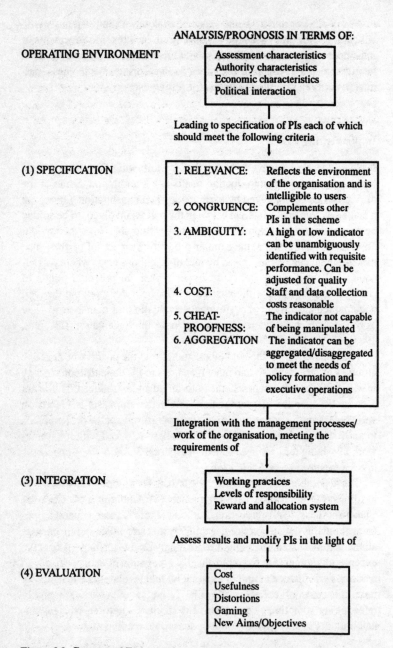

Figure 8.3: Conceptual Framework

The prescriptive point is that the best combination of PI characteristics can only be determined with reference to the context in which they are going to be used. The framework for performance measurement suggested here starts not with the selection of indicators meeting certain criteria but with a prior stage of analysis leading to their specification. This contextual placing of PIs is best done with reference to a close study of the operating environment of the organisation - the absence of which gives rise to many of the problems identified in studies of PIs. This process involves close consideration of four inter-related sets of characteristics.

(1) *Assessment Characteristics*

The sources and nature of evaluation systems being used - for example, managerial, scientific, professional - and points of conflict or complementarity.

(2) *Authority Characteristics*

The sources of authority with which an evaluation process is validated and sanctioned. This in turn influences the mode of evaluation and use to which data are put - for accountability, control or development purposes.

(3) *Economic Characteristics*

The emphasis placed on various components of efficiency, for example efficiency in production rather than efficiency in consumption. The first of the two Es attempts to measure the former while Effectiveness and the related question of the right mix of outputs concern the latter. The emphasis placed on the various components will reflect some view of priorities attached to the problems facing the organisation.

(4) *Political Interaction*

The relationship between evaluation mechanisms and interaction among stake holders, interest groups and other public institutions involved in evaluation.

As our study of local government described above shows, the counter-productive effects of measurement schemes arose mainly from lack of analysis under these headings, preceding the specification of indicators. In the Planning Department, for example, it was assumed that the professional and managerial forms of assessment could co-exist; yet the latter became dominant, as analysis of the political interaction and associated authority characteristics might have indicated. These would also have shown a longer run shift, already underway, in the influence of pressure groups from business interests towards those of residents. As concern mounted about environmental issues in the area, the processes of public consultation and the judgement of planning professionals assumed greater importance. This is not to suggest that simply by analysing the features listed here a perfect set of indicators will emerge. What the analysis does provide is a realistic set of guidelines within which the process of selection and negotiation about indicators can proceed.

Integration - Evaluation

Because they can change the way in which people work, evaluation schemes must be combined or integrated with an organisation in such a way as to strengthen rather than inhibit the best features of its working practices. One of the most common failings with performance measurement is a lack of careful management at the integration and post-integration stages. This can be seen from studies of the introduction and application of PIs in contexts as diverse as Soviet manufacturing industry and American public service (Pollitt, 1989) which would suggest a typical performance indicator 'cycle' as in Figure 8.4.

Starting from some crisis, perhaps accompanied by a change in authority figures, the desire for new measures to make the system more accountable is awakened. Once launched this moves through various phases - Agenda to Improvement - in which PIs are chosen and as a result

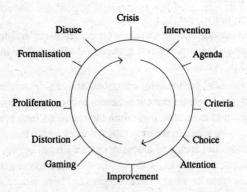

Figure 8.4

of attention and management action show an early improvement in performance. As obvious improvements are exhausted and managers get a better understanding of how the indicators work, there is an incentive to manipulate the system to maintain the required rate of improvement. This 'gaming', as seen in our case study, most frequently takes the form of attention to measured activities at the expense of tasks which are less well defined or measured. Attempts to correct this distortion can lead to a proliferation of indicators, in a formalised and complex system which is so difficult to understand that it falls into disuse, as attention shifts to other concerns within the organisation.

The avoidance of this cycle and the fruitful integration of PIs with working practices must be based on careful observation of the way in which an organisation operates. When looking at organisations to see how PIs can be incorporated, the following distinctions are helpful:

(a) the formal structure - the role relationships set out in the organisation chart, which, because of the dynamics of an organisation, are rarely correctly defined and seldom followed;

(b) the assumed structure - the situation as it is assumed to be by the individuals in the organisation, which can influence the way it works;

(c) the extant structure - the actual nature of the organisation as revealed by a systematic exploration and analysis;

(d) the requisite structure - the organisation as it needs to be, in a given context, to meet needs most appropriately.

These distinctions avoid the formal/informal categories used by the human relations school, regarded by some organisational analysts (Rowbottom, 1973; Jaques, 1989) as confusing. The failure to integrate PIs successfully often arises because these distinctions are ignored. In the case study, for example, the PI system was incorrectly based on (a) and (b) rather than (c) and (d), which resulted in a measurement system appropriate for the hierarchy of a military command but quite inappropriate for a department of town planners.

Close analysis of an organisation along these lines helps to ensure that the measurement system is compatible with three key aspects of its operations:

(1) *Responsibility* - the judgement expected of decision making units and individuals at different levels within an organisation.

(2) *Timing* - information available within the time scale necessary for decision making.

(3) *Allocation* - the system of incentives and priorities which determines the allocation of resources, remuneration and opportunities to individuals and groups.

A tighter system of performance measurement may, for example, reduce an individual's scope for discretion for the conduct of work to a level below the capacity to exercise it. The response to the frustration caused by this might be some attempt at enlargement of responsibilities or moving out of the job. Although this might be desirable, it may be an unintended consequence.

Inappropriate timing of reviews of the performance of individuals and groups may have a similar counterproductive effect on the exercise of responsibility. Many PI systems are linked with the budgetary cycle. Monitoring by some arbitrary accounting period may provide an unsuitable assessment for the management of a project extending over longer time scales. This relates to the point raised above concerning the distinction of PIs for different purposes - accountability, control and development. The timing of indicators for one function may be quite inappropriate for another.

Since PIs provide evidence of performance, they inevitably influence resource allocation. It is therefore essential that different groups of indicators bear upon allocation decisions in a clear and consistent manner. Among the questions that should be asked here are the following: How do indicator systems used at Departmental level relate to those used in the process of corporate planning and management? Is the role of indicators simply to establish an agenda for the discussion of priorities for resource allocation, or is it to determine exactly how these decisions are made?

Finally, unless performance measurement schemes are themselves subjected to performance measurement the 'indicator cycle' will recur. All schemes must include some self-evaluation process, not only to assess costs and benefits but also to incorporate new aims and objectives. Many public sector organisations are undergoing change and are in the process of trying to discover exactly what their objectives are. This is a crucial part of their activities which is not reflected in performance indicators. Because there was an inadequate process of evaluation in the local authority Departments included in our study, the choice of PIs tended to reduce flexibility and consequently the capacity for learning and change, which should have been included as part of a significant cluster of performance indicators.

Concluding Comments

In an influential article which coincided with the change in attitudes to public sector efficiency, the American public sector economist, Mancur Olson (1974) observed, 'It is essential to remember that a bad job of evaluating the output of the public sector may bring extraordinary increases in efficiency, if before the bad evaluation there was no evaluation at all'. As we enter the 1990s this view is being promoted by some with almost crusading zeal. Every self-respecting institution is expected to have performance indicators. In some organisations the quantity of performance indicators is a performance indicator in itself. However, there is substantial evidence with which to challenge the view that any indicators are better than none. This chapter has argued that if the 'bad job' of evaluation is done with PIs that are not set firmly in the appropriate organisational context, performance measurement may provoke hostile attitudes and become counterproductive.

There can be no doubt that the public sector needs PIs, but if they are to have coherence and meaning they must be based on a close analysis of how public sector institutions operate and reflect what they are really trying to do. Thus PIs must not become simply devices used in a static situation to maximise outputs and reduce costs but also must assist in the measurement of change and the development of capacities of individuals and organisations. If measurement systems are to do this they must reflect the content of work and levels of responsibility within an organisation. Too frequently measurement systems are introduced without any reference to these elements. In such cases they can be harmful.

References

Argyris, C., (1962), *International Competence Organisational Effectiveness*, Tavistock Publications.

Bichard, R., (1989), 'Managing Professionals in Local Government', *EFMD Barcelona*.

Blau, P. M., and Scott, W. R., (1963), *Formal Organisations*, Routledge & Kegan Paul.

Caplow, T., (1964), *The Sociology of Work*, McGraw-Hill.

Carter, N., (1989), 'Performance Indicators: "Backseat Driving" and "Hands Off" Control', *Policy and Politics* 2, 131-8.

Cave, M., Hanney, S., Kogan, M., and Trevett, G., (1988), *The Use of Performance Indicators in Higher Education*, Jessica Kingsley Publishers.

Fletcher, C., and Williams, R., (1985), *Performance Appraisal and Career Development*, Hutchinson.

Hughes, E., (1981), 'Accountants as Professionals', in Esland, *People and Work*, Open University.

Jaques, E., (1989), *Requisite Organisation*, Gower, Aldershot.

Knight, K., (1989), 'Performance Indicators and the Organisation', *Brunel Seminar for the Royal Borough of Kingston-upon-Thames*.

Lupton, T., (1983), *Management and the Social Sciences*, Penguin, London.

Olson, M., (1974), 'On the Priority of Public Problems', in Marris, R., *The Corporate Society*, Macmillan, London.

Pollitt, C., (1986), 'Beyond the Managerial Model', *Financial Accountability and Management*, Vol. 2, No. 3, Autumn.

Pollitt, C., (1989), 'Performance Indicators in the Public Services: The Time Dimension', *Brunel University Seminar*.

Rowbottom, R., (1973), *Hospital Organisation*, Heinemann, London.

Williams, A., (1985), *Performance Measurement in the Public Sector: Paving the Road to Hell?*, Arthur Young Lecture, Department of Accounting, University of Glasgow.

Chapter 9

Evaluating Performance in the Department of the Environment

Peter Daffern and Grahame Walshe*

Introduction

This chapter describes in outline aspects of performance measurement (PM) in one central government department. The question of how typical the department is lies beyond the scope of this paper but we can say that the Department of the Environment (DOE) has responsibility for a range of 'businesses' or activities as well as policy-making and administrative functions. It is important to recognise that changes have occurred in recent years in the nature of the DOE's responsibilities and that what follows is based on the situation as it existed in November 1989. But despite the changes certain general underlying features remain undisturbed. In particular, it may be said that *control* over performance represents a continuum, reflecting the degree of *directness* of control or influence. As a consequence, indicators or measures of performance span a substantial range of complexity. These ideas were previously explored by Heigham (1988), but to illustrate them, consider the following examples.

Some activities are more or less completely *internal* to the department, and hence directly controlled. As well as activities such as typing and reprographics which produce outputs which are intermediate, i.e. become inputs to other activities, these services include answering correspondence from the public and producing replies to Parliamentary Questions. In assessing performance in such areas, measures or indicators are reasonably straightforward. At the other end of the spectrum, some responsibilities of the department are exercised through sponsored bodies. Moreover, the activities of these sponsored bodies may be purely

---

* The views expressed here are those of the authors alone and not of their Departments.

permissive in nature or do no more than encourage or facilitate others to undertake tasks. An illustration is the work of English Heritage which receives applications from private owners of listed buildings for grants towards certain works of restoration. Even where grants are approved, there is no guarantee that they will be taken up, or that the works will be undertaken. In such situations, the Department's influence is much less direct, and indicators of performance for DOE or English Heritage become more complex.

These features - a continuum of directness of control, and a corresponding range of complexity - apply to many organisations, and certainly to other government departments. The same may be said of the underlying concepts which allow the development of practical performance measures. These are well known and so will not be rehearsed in detail here. However, it is useful to recall one or two key aspects of the model implicit in the approach adopted.

Value for money (VFM) can be formally represented by the following expression:

		Value of Output	x	Actual Output	x	Planned Output	x	Planned Input	x	Actual Input
VFM =										
		Actual Output		Planned Output		Planned Input		Actual Input		Value of Input

or symbolically:

$$VFM = \frac{V.Q}{Q} \times \frac{Q}{Q'} \times \frac{Q'}{N'} \times \frac{N'}{N} \times \frac{N}{C.N}$$

In this expression Q is output, N is input, the superscript represents a planned input or output and V and C are weights, values or prices attaching, respectively, to Q and N. It is in the first and last of these ratios that the difference between public and private sectors is found. In particular, V and C are invariably represented in the private sector by market prices. In the public sector, they tend to be the result of political decisions and find published expression in documents such as the Public Expenditure White Paper (PEWP) and sponsored bodies' corporate plans.

It is clear that the search for allocative and technical efficiency is as central to the concern of government departments as to profit-making private enterprises. (For a discussion of these concepts of efficiency see Chapter 3 above.) Guidance on the role of performance measurement in securing technical efficiency is set out (in draft form) in HM Treasury

(1988). In terms of the definitions used in the Treasury guidance, Q/Q' may be seen as representing effectiveness, N'/N economy and Q'/N' planned efficiency. The ratio Q/N (i.e. Q/Q' x Q'/N' x N'/N) is an *ex post* measure of achieved technical efficiency.

In DOE, performance measurement (PM) is integral to specific processes through which technical and allocative efficiency are sought. Externally the Public Expenditure Survey (PES) seeks not only to reconcile existing policies and commitments with new ones but also to promote improvements in efficiency. Finance divisions in DOE ask policy divisions (in March of each year) to submit output and performance measures and expenditure targets in the previous few years, together with material on spending increases and decreases and their likely effects in the future. Through the subsequent months, bids from all departments are assembled by the Treasury, discussed in bilaterals between the Department and the Treasury and agreed. After the broad outlines are published (in the Autumn Statement), the Departmental booklet of the PEWP, published in January, sets out the Department's aims, how the spending programmes further its aims, how its resources are divided between its programmes, and what it plans to achieve with its spending, compared with achievements and performance against targets in previous years. In the course of this process a substantial body of PM information on programmes is thus assembled. The Department is responsible for its running costs as well as for programme expenditure. As part of the survey the Department prepares a management efficiency plan (MEP) in which assessments are made of changes in efficiency over the past year, and in which proposals are set out for achieving further gains in efficiency. For this purpose, a total factor productivity index has been derived for a substantial proportion of the administrative processes of the Department.

One wholly internal approach to securing value for money is the MINIS round. MINIS (Management Information System for Ministers) is the Department's top management information system. It is an annual stocktaking covering objectives, assessment of past performance(particularly against targets) and proposed future objectives, tasks and targets. It is designed to enable senior management and ministers to assess the Department's progress and performance.

In addition to these regular reporting procedures which incorporate periodic PM, the Department is continuing development of appropriate policy evaluation methods which can contribute to and complement PM in MINIS and the PES round.

The remaining sections of this chapter are largely concerned with PM in different aspects of the Department's areas of responsibility. The Department's programme expenditure is considered. At an even greater distance from direct control, PM in the Department's sponsored bodies is examined, and some concluding thoughts are offered. The final section is concerned with the area where tightest control is exercised - over technical efficiency in the use of the DOE's own administrative resources.

Administrative Performance in a Total Factor Productivity Context

The proportion of departmental funding spent on internal administrative processes is relatively small - in the case of Environment it is less than five per cent. Nevertheless, the attractions of doing work on performance measurement in this area are clear. First, good practice should begin at home. Second, control over outputs and inputs is greater than with much of programme spending so that the potential for improving efficiency as a result of PM is real. Third, methodological lessons obtained with in-house work may be applied elsewhere - for example, in the numerous organisations and bodies sponsored by the DOE. Finally, if one can demonstrate to other departments the successful employment of a PM tool then diffusion throughout the service may reap wider benefits: a department should not be guilty of thinking that, because the home side can only score a handful of goals, the game is not worth playing.

The initial impetus for such work came from two sources. First, a Treasury requirement to produce a Management Efficiency Plan - which would achieve efficiency increase of at least 1.5 per cent per annum - provided one external stimulus. Second, in the mid-1980s researchers were beginning to attempt productivity measurement in private sector service organisations (for example, Levitt, 1986) with interesting results. Various ideal forms of measurement were entertained; the structure of the index eventually employed owes something to work by Molyneux and Thompson (1987). The index is a current-weighted index of the form:

$$TFPI_t = \frac{\sum_{i=1}^{n} O_{it} W_{it}}{\sum_{i=1}^{m} O_{io} W_{it}} \Bigg/ \frac{\sum_{i=1}^{n} RC_{it} + \sum_{i=1}^{n} CC_{it}}{P_t}$$

The total factor productivity index (TFPI) value for the current period (t) is thus derived from:

(a) Outputs: $O_{it}^{\wedge}$ is the output index value for the ith activity in period t; it is weighted by an expenditure weight $(W_{it}^{\wedge})$ for activity i in period t. $O_{io}^{\wedge}$ is the quantity index value for the ith activity in the base period; in the Paasche formulation it is currently weighted $(W_{it}^{\wedge})$ by expenditure. M outputs are used in the calculation where m is less than n - the total of costed activities.

(b) Inputs: Index values for costs appear in the denominator. These current costs for all (n) activities cover both running costs (RC) and computer capital costs (CC) for the ith activity in period t. Current costs are deflated by an index of factor prices $(P_t^{\wedge})$.

For those who find it helpful to have such abstract concepts exemplified, Table 9.1 has been devised to show how such an index may be constructed. The Paasche form of the index ensures that the productivity record is

Table 9.1: Example of a Productivity Index, Three Outputs, 1984-85 to 1988-89

		84/85	85/86	86/87	87/88	88/89	88/89 Weights
1	Output 1:N	710	735	750	775	797	£1.25m
2	Output 2:N	220	225	230	235	240	£0.64m
3	Output 3:N	550	440	580	450	610	£0.87m
4	Index 1	100	103.5	105.6	109.2	112.3	.4529
5	Index 2	100	102.3	104.5	106.8	109.1	.2319
6	Index 3	100	80.0	105.5	81.8	110.9	.3125
7	Aggregate Output Index	100	95.8	105.3	100.0	111.1	
8	Inputs	110.1	115.3	120.2	123.1	132.5	
9	Input prices	100.0	104.4	108.2	111.3	116.7	
10	Inputs/prices	110.1	110.4	111.1	110.6	113.5	
11	Index of Inputs	100.0	100.3	100.9	100.4	103.1	
12	Output/Input	100.0	95.5	104.3	99.6	107.8	

Average Annual percentage increase in output = 1.90%
Average Annual percentage increase in input = 0.76%
Average Annual change in productivity index = 1.14%

Notes
(i) The decimalised output weights in the final column are constrained to equal 1.0.
(ii) In row 8 several factor input values have been aggregated in order to simplify presentation.

observed through the lens of the current resource allocation pattern. This is clearly desirable in a Department where changes in priorities can achieve significant shifts of emphasis in the medium term.

There are several notable features of the index which are worth discussing before we move on to PM in the wider setting of programme spending:

- output composition and the sampling pattern;
- cost coverage and in particular how capital costs are assessed;
- the choice of cost deflator;
- the DOE record on productivity change.

Let us look at each of these in turn.

Outputs

The TFPI outputs are indexed physical measures of output - library loans, typing pool throughputs, planning applications dealt with, rent assessment panel cases, photocopies produced, written and oral Parliamentary Questions answered, statistical forms processed, invoices handled, etc. These outputs represent:

(a) the routine activities of a large and complex service organisation;

(b) casework and processing operations peculiar to DOE.

An example of the former is 'Archive Feet Cleared', which may conjure up an image of artificial limbs being tested for robustness but is, in fact, a measure of the progress achieved by archivists with the job of weeding out redundant files. An example of the latter is 'Chimney Height Appeals Processed' - that is, appeals by companies against the statutorily-determined height of industrial smokestacks - a series which could not be included in the sample because of its extreme variability and relatively low demands on resources. It is important to note that no allowance is yet made in the index for the improving quality of output, for example where reductions of turnaround times are achieved in certain casework areas. About 60 per cent of the weight in the output index is contributed by casework activities with the remainder accounted for by routine volume processing operations.

Coverage of the Department's administrative undertakings is not complete, and never can be. Hence it is necessary to question how comprehensive and representative the sample is. The number of activities actually monitored in the 1989 version of the TFPI was 170, and the proportion of employees covered by the output index is approximately

50 per cent. The assumption made in deploying these output data in the index is that they are a proxy for the true administrative output series. That is, those administrative outputs which it will always be difficult to quantify - for example, the outputs of the legal directorate (drafting bills and statutory instruments, contesting court cases, providing opinions on powers), ministerial briefings, the production of statistical reports, drafting and producing press releases, and so on - are assumed to be growing at approximately the same aggregate rate as the sample outputs.

It is, of course, difficult to entertain the notion that the half of the Department monitored in the TFPI is in some sense atypical. All the large directorates are reasonably well represented and the few small directorates which are under-represented (the legal and information directorates for example) are unlikely all to have sustained a growth rate markedly different from the average. It is likely that the excluded series exhibit different growth rates, some higher and some lower than the average already estimated, and that they tend to offset one another. The additions made each year to the output index will probably not alter the impression of steady, if not spectacular, growth.

It is appropriate to close this section with a note on the weights employed. 'Revenue' weights would be the ideal to aim at, but they would require price data which are not common (nor indeed, always acceptable) in the public sector. However, if resources are allocated efficiently, then the following Paretian-type condition will hold:

$$\frac{MVa}{MCa} = \frac{MVb}{MCb} = \ \text{.......} \ \frac{MVn}{MCn}$$

In this expression MV is marginal value and MC is marginal cost, while a, b, ...n are activity outputs. It is clear that no increase in value can be obtained from a reallocation of resources once this condition is observed; hence it is an optimum. If it is obtained, marginal costs in such ratios (note that the condition only requires that the ratios are equal) can be employed as proxies for marginal values or 'prices'. In other words, administrative resource decisions may be used to reach an underlying valuation of output: it is assumed that the value of output is at least equal to the resources allocated to producing it; or that the marginal value of output is proportional to its marginal cost.

It is seldom worth creating departmental accounting systems which would give precise expenditure data for each activity (the divisions and branches making up directorates are the basic accounting units in DOE) and, consequently, employment weights have been initially employed in the TFPI. Employment numbers are readily available from the MINIS and are a useful proxy for expenditure data. This approach will be refined as resources permit.

Inputs

The input variable in the indexed real values of gross running costs including wages and salaries, office rents, computer bureaux fees, stationery and other materials, training, and the acquisition of minor office machines. In addition, an estimate has been made of the replacement cost of information technology (IT) capital equipment used during the year. Thus all the obvious costs, both current and capital, have been covered in the calculation of the index.

The estimate of 'quasi-rentals' for computer usage deserves a brief discussion. Significant DOE investment in computers built up during the second half of the 1970s; bought-in bureau services were the main computer resource before the installation of departmental IT. Hence, given that the TFPI index starts in 1984-85, and that the life of a computer is usually assumed to be fairly short (four or five years is a typical commercial assumption), it was assumed that capital spending on IT before 1980 was fully depreciated by 1984-85. Clearly, this was not wholly accurate, but making that assumption could not occasion grave error.

There are two main steps in the calculation:

(a) Estimating the annual charge that would be made, under conditions of competition, for the computers installed. This rental charge may be estimated from:

- the price of IT;
- the rate at which capital is likely to wear out;
- the cost of tying up capital in IT.

In other words, computer price levels, rates of depreciation, and interest rates are inputs to the calculation.

(b) In practice, rentals are revised to take account of inflation, hence the sums estimated in (a) need to reflect replacement costs in the appropriate sector of the computer industry. This is impossible because trends in computer prices are not published. However, the Business Monitor series on *Costs for the Radio and Electronic Capital Goods Industry*, which must relate in some degree to prices in the computer sector, is employed to adjust for this factor.

Clearly, the same method can be used to provide quasi-rentals for other items of capital equipment. But it was not thought worthwhile to estimate rentals for miscellaneous items of, say, office furniture. Spending on such capital assets is proxied fairly well by other components in running costs.

Deflating Costs

Some resources have been spent on the construction of a price series suitable for deflating the index of costs to a constant price, or real terms, basis. The candidates for inclusion in such a deflator series are:

(a) public sector pay: about three-fifths of running costs are incurred in the form of wages and salaries;

(b) PSA rentals: running costs include a significant element for office rents;

(c) the retail price index: because prices of materials and various office requisites are probably well tracked by this series;

(d) capital goods prices: it is not immediately obvious what combination of published series might be pressed into service here.

In the event, preliminary estimates have suggested that the use of the GDP deflator does not entail a great sacrifice in accuracy. Nevertheless, there is a commitment to refine the estimates in this component of the calculation.

The Record

There is still some way to go before estimates of productivity change calculated in this way can be treated with total confidence. Although output coverage has increased to 170 series in 1989, and although the input index covers all the significant factors of production, there are still areas of DOE work which remain relatively under-represented in the index. Moreover, there is further work to do in establishing a credible deflator for the input series. Bearing those caveats in mind, Figures 9.1 and 9.2 show how estimated TFPI for the DOE has changed since 1984-85.

One must be wary of interpreting the year-to-year changes in these series too literally. Productivity series, except those for the largest national aggregates, typically show very uneven movements from year to year. The moderately smooth increases in productivity associated with macro-economic growth are built up by aggregating together very much more irregular series for individual enterprises and activities. The trend

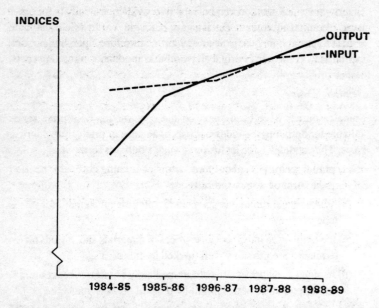

Figure 9.1: DOE Administrative Inputs and Outputs

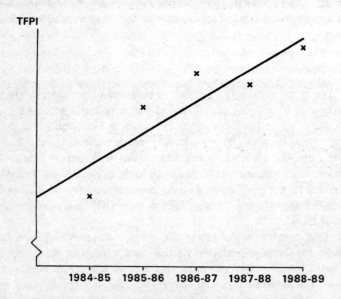

Figure 9.2: DOE Total Factor Productivity Index

of growth at the lower level of activity explored here can only be assessed over a number of years taken together. Bearing that in mind, the DOE record of productivity improvement, an increase of about four per cent per annum, compares favourably with other reported results for service sector productivity change (Levitt, 1986; Levitt and Joyce, 1987; Smith, 1989).

As for the future, the continuity of the series will be affected by the addition of new data which will tend to reduce comparability with earlier years. Thus there is a trade-off between extending the coverage of the index across DOE and the ability to make comparisons over more than three or four years. A further loss in continuity is likely to arise because of the separation of some service functions common to the Departments of Environment and Transport. Numerous administrative outputs have not been recorded historically on a separate departmental basis, so where realistic apportionment of totals is not possible, the data for earlier years may have to be disregarded.

Performance Measurement in Programme Expenditure

It was noted earlier that PM is an important element in the monitoring, evaluation, review and planning of programme expenditure through the Public Expenditure Survey (PES) and MINIS processes. Attention will be focussed here on the former. In the 1989 PES round, measures of performance were provided in 58 policy fields. In order to illustrate the types of measures which have been devised, and some of the difficulties which attend PM in programme expenditure, a brief examination is made of two programme areas: Derelict Land Clearance and Estate Action.

The return made by a division responsible for a particular programme area in the 1989 PES round was a completed *pro forma* with five basic sections:

A Aims

B Objectives

C Inputs

D Outputs

E Performance Measures, subdivided into three:

    (1) Efficiency

    (2) Effectiveness

(3) Economy

For sections C, D and E, a return should have comprised figures for planned and actual levels for each of the past four years (including forecast actuals in the case of the current i.e. 'last' year); and planned levels for the next three years. Each *pro forma* sets aside space for a commentary, or PM narrative, so that inferences which can be drawn from the data, or shortcomings of the estimates, may be properly understood. It is evident from the returns that in many fields few measurements of economy have been devised and that often economy has been subsumed within efficiency.

Derelict Land Reclamation

The main aim of this programme is:

'To promote the reclamation for beneficial use of land which is derelict, neglected or unsightly, by the payment of grant to local authorities and other public bodies, and to private persons and organisations.'

Reference is also made in the aims to the scale of the problem and what might be expected to occur in the absence of programme expenditure. Some of the objectives of the programme are sufficiently well-defined to be regarded as targets, which are given greater precision in the PM entries. They include targets:

'to reclaim at least 2710 hectares of derelict land in the period 1990-91 to 1992-93, 50 per cent of which will be for hard-end uses;

to devote between 25 per cent and 30 per cent of derelict land grant resources in each year to reclamation schemes in the inner cities;

to devote at least £6m per year to limestone work in the West Midlands'.

Inputs are defined simply as expenditure, and outputs as the number of hectares of reclaimed land in total, sub-divided into 'hard' and 'soft' end uses, the former embracing industry, housing, etc., and the latter green space, agriculture, and so on.

Performance measures follow from the earlier elements of the return. Efficiency is measured in terms of the average cost per hectare of completed schemes, in aggregate, and for hard and soft end uses separately. Effectiveness is assessed in terms of total land reclaimed as a proportion of the target; the proportion reclaimed for hard end use is also made the subject of an effectiveness measure. For Inner City areas specifically, there is a measure of total expenditure (both local authority and non-local authority) as a proportion of the total figure; and a measure of land reclaimed as a proportion of total land reclaimed. For coalfield reclamation, the target and performance measure is the proportion of expenditure; while for limestone reclamation it is simply the amount spent in £m. The only measure of economy is a negative one: the amount of value recovered from the site sale in £m; although typical leverage rates (that is, the ratio of non-grant funding to grant funding) are also noted. It would be too costly to produce figures on a more comprehensive basis, and the idea of following the progress of a sample of schemes to arrive at typical figures does at least give some feel for the sort of leverage being achieved.

Estate Action (EA)

The main aims of this programme are:

(a) to widen tenure choices and improve the quality of service for residents of run-down council housing estates;

(b) to assist local authorities to revitalise run-down housing estates through innovatory measures involving diversity of tenure;

(c) to promote comprehensive and bespoke solutions to tackling problems on run-down estates;

(d) to demonstrate the cost-effectiveness of these measures.

The objectives include promotion of diversity of tenure, and support for greater tenant control on a larger proportion of schemes; together with a number of specified improvements to dimensions of management, such as 'increase (by 10 per cent) rental incomes through more efficient management'.

Measures of two inputs are provided: additional allocations in £m, and the number of staff in the central EA team. A considerable array of outputs is listed, including several which derive relatively clearly from aims/objectives, such as schemes in progress and started, numbers of dwellings being improved, disposals to the private sector and empty dwellings brought back into use for the homeless. However, others also include number of new community refurbishment schemes (CRS) and additional jobs and training places created through CRS and other estate-based initiatives.

Amongst the performance measures, economy is represented by a figure showing the input of EA resources as a percentage of total public expenditure on new schemes. Only two measures of effectiveness had been used up to 1988-89:

(a) percentage of new schemes involving disposals to the private sector;

(b) the number of tenant management committees and estate management boards in new schemes.

A number of additional measures have been developed, some of which reflect intermediate outputs, for example the take-up of right-to-buy and reduction in empty dwellings. Other measures relate to tenant satisfaction (through turnover rates and transfer requests); or are concerned with broader social effects - for example, the percentage of schemes where there are reductions in the amount of crime and vandalism. The data base for these latter is currently being developed.

Four measures of efficiency are provided, three of which are: the unit cost per dwelling of new schemes, the allocations of resources per new CRS, and the unit cost of empty dwellings brought back into use for the homeless. A fourth measure is the cost per additional job or training place created in the CRS programme.

Commentary on the Results

PM for programme expenditure in DOE reflects both the problems inherent in such expenditures in any central government department, and the pace and particular form adopted for PM in DOE. Among the former, stress has been laid on the directness of control or influence which the Department exercises. This has a number of implications for the practice of PM. These include a need to measure administrative efficiency in many programme areas so as to ensure satisfactory performance in those aspects of the overall process which are within direct control; and the need not only to develop measures of programme performance which appropriately reflect the interaction of several influences on outcomes, but also to ensure that the scope for narrative commentary on the PM return is properly appreciated and utilised by those completing it.

In the case of Estate Action, for example, the commentary in the latest return points out that the programme is increasingly focussing on a few large and problematic estates and that as a consequence it is difficult to make meaningful comparisons between years on the basis of the volume of schemes or dwellings completed.

This, in turn, suggests a broader problem with the use of time series in programme PM: the changing nature of aims and objectives. In the case of EA, the addition of the CRS during the currency of the programme and the understandable desire to secure cost-effective job creation under the scheme have necessarily meant a recasting of the measures of performance. In the case of derelict land clearance the emphasis on hard end use has tended to vary through time. For both of these programmes, there has also been, to some extent at least, a tendency for the 'best' projects (i.e. those most likely to be cost effective) to be undertaken first, leaving the more intractable and hence more expensive problems for later years. Series on efficiency will inevitably reflect that sequence of project implementation.

DOE has claims to be considered one of the departments most enthusiastically developing PM as a part of the systematic approach to management. Nonetheless, the rate at which PM concepts are refined and can be diffused throughout the Department is necessarily constrained by resource availabilities. Further development continues both within central finance divisions and (in the form of more sophisticated returns) within policy divisions. Needless to say, the scope for further improvement remains significant.

PM in programme expenditure for the PES process must be seen as one aspect of the range of methods by which Ministers and senior management seek to assure themselves that the performance of the department is adequately monitored and reviewed. Others most closely related are:

(a) MINIS, which annually assesses performance and sets targets for directorates within the Department;

(b) policy evaluation which is used on an ad hoc basis to assess whether and to what extent (and how cost-effectively) individual policy initiatives have fulfilled their objectives.

The parallels with an appropriate system of PM for programme expenditure are clear.

Arm's Length Performance: Non-Departmental Public Bodies

DOE sponsors a substantial number of bodies in diverse fields. Although these bodies have their own boards and produce their own corporate plans, performance in them could obviously never be a matter of indifference to the Department. There are substantial parallels in the case of the Department's agencies, but the focus here will be on the non-departmental public bodies (NDPBs) for which it is responsible. The nature of the relationship between a government department and one of its NDPBs is clearly a complex one, which is beyond the scope of this discussion. One or two aspects of that relationship do, however, bear upon performance measurement.

The first of these concerns the nature and functions of an NDPB, which will typically act both as adviser to the relevant Secretary of State, in which role it is a (or the) repository of expert knowledge in a defined field of responsibility, and as advocate of additional spending on the activities in that field of responsibility. This is at least suggests the possibility of a divergence of view between 'owners' (the department) and managers as to what constitute appropriate objectives for the NDPB, and hence what constitute appropriate measures of performance. It is, however, worth recalling the distinction between technical and allocative efficiency. The former is a necessary (though not sufficient) condition for economic efficiency and is represented by the three physical ratios of the value for money formula given at page 144 above. The other two ratios in the vfm formula are discussed in the deliberations preceding the preparation of the corporate plan, and in negotiations which result in the determination of the level of resources available to the NDPB.

The second aspect concerns the various dimensions of performance. Essentially these appear to divide into two:

(a) the performance of the Department as sponsor;

(b) the performance of the NDPB itself.

However, there will in practice be considerable overlap between these two dimensions. Some aspects of departmental performance can be separated out and measured with comparative ease: for example, those aspects which may be classed as purely 'administrative' and which are of interest in dealings with all of a department's sponsored bodies, such as turnaround times for correspondence, deadlines for financial submissions on behalf of the NDPB, and so on. Other aspects of sponsorship are, however, inextricably intertwined with the performance of the NDPB itself. These include:

(a) the selection of appropriate personnel to head the NDPB; negotiation and agreement of key objectives for the NDPB to be incorporated in the corporate plan;

(b) the existence of appropriate mechanisms within the NDPB, and between the Department and the NDPB, to ensure propriety, regularity and value for money in the spending of the resources allocated to the NDPB. Clearly, the last of these will embrace an appropriate system of PM for the NDPB itself.

The activities of an NDPB, like those of a department, will normally lend themselves to a distinction between measures relating to 'administration' and the 'real world', though this is hard to sustain in some cases. For the former, we would expect measures to be employed which are similar to those used in departments. As with departments, performance in activities with real world outcomes will tend to be more difficult to measure as control or influence becomes less direct; this will lead to an increasing complexity of indicators.

To illustrate these and other issues, there follows a brief consideration of performance measurement approaches in two NDPBs sponsored by DOE: the Housing Corporation (HC) and English Heritage (EH). The discussion is based upon the 1989 corporate plans of the two organisations.

Performance Measurement in the Housing Corporation

The aim of the Housing Corporation has been defined as:

> 'To support the social housing sector by working with housing associations and others in England to provide good homes for those in housing need.' (Housing Corporation Corporate Plan, 1989)

Certain prerequisites for the achievement of this aim are set out, and it is then translated into a series of main strategy components. In implementing the strategy the HC adopts a set of organisational goals. The remainder of the corporate plan is devoted to working out the overall aims and objectives for each of the HC's main groups of activities through:

(a) identification of key and sub-objectives;

(b) reviews of past performance and assessment of issues of future importance;

(c) presentation of resource assumptions and options for expenditure programmes;

(d) setting out targets for the next two years.

Constraints of space preclude a full exploration of the approach of the HC to performance measurement. However, some brief examples will serve to illustrate the types of measure identified.

The first main group of activities is concerned with providing funds to invest in housing where the key objective is 'to secure the maximum investment of funds and to target and manage those funds to secure the maximum impact on priority housing needs' (HC Corporate Plan, 1989, p 9). One of the sub-objectives is to maximise funds for capital investment by housing associations (HAs), and one of the suggested targets contributing to the achievement of this aim is an increase in the proportion of approvals on a mixed-funded basis. Within the second group of activities, providing grants to support housing association activities, many of the sub-objectives are to provide new arrangements for grant, schemework, audit and special needs housing by target dates. Again the indicators are relatively straightforward milestones.

A third group of activities is related to the second: promoting effective management by housing associations. Here a fairly heterogeneous array of sub-objectives is provided: from an outcome measure (promotion of tenant satisfaction) to detailed elements of effective management by HAs, for example reinforcing the registration process to strengthen new associations. The latter generates fairly specific targets, such as:

'all regularly funded new HAs to achieve mixed-funded status within six years';

'75 per cent of regularly funded new HAs to achieve a stock of 250 dwellings in five years'. (HC Corporate Plan, 1989, p. 55)

These targets suggest fairly straightforward indicators. But the tenant satisfaction sub-objective spawns a mixture of targets, some with reasonably clear and directly related indicators, and others where the indicators are clear but do not obviously reflect progress towards targets.

A fourth main group of activities is intended to assist tenants' choice but this is largely promotional in nature and is of very recent origin, so that indicators have yet to be developed.

The final section of the plan relates to the internal operation of the corporation - its management and resourcing - and as such tends to echo the objectives and performance measurement found in the Department's own administrative work.

Performance Measurement in English Heritage (EH)

There are some similarities between the HC and EH in their approach to performance measurement. A statement of role and aims is translated into four key corporate objectives to achieve:

(a) knowledge of the need for action in the historic environment;

(b) a structure for EH which improves effectiveness and efficiency;

(c) a Properties in Care estate which is well repaired, efficiently managed, continues to earn an increasing per centage of total costs and makes maximum use of external resources;

(d) a better general understanding of EH's role.

As with the Housing Corporation, these are in turn divided for implementation into three groups, concerned respectively with Conservation, Properties in Care and Central Services. Each of these three groups has its own set of objectives for several categories of work; and for each category, targets and performance indicators are listed. Targets and indicators for the Conservation and Properties in Care groups include some relating both to outcomes and to administrative measures while the Central Services group only has the latter type of measure.

Lack of space precludes detailed discussion of EH performance indicators but examples of targets are:

(a) one activity of the Conservation Group follows from the power to make grants in London to any historic building. Here the target is administrative: to make 80 per cent of offers of Grants within four months of the receipt of completed applications;

(b) for the Properties in Care Group, timetables are set out for major improvements to certain properties - targets relate to achieving milestones within budget;

(c) also for the Properties in Care Group, there are financial targets including: membership to reach 209,000 and a total marketing income of £8.5m by specified dates.

Indicators follow fairly readily from these targets.

Commentary on the Results

Performance measurement and, indeed, corporate planning, are at various stages of development in the NDPBs sponsored by DOE. As might be expected NDPBs encounter many of the problems which the Department itself faces in PM work. These difficulties arise from a variety of sources. In part they reflect the basis for their existence, which usually derives from the fact that the outputs they produce are often public goods or have external effects on the community. In part they follow from the nature of the relationship they have with the Department.

Within the Department, consideration is currently being given to this relationship and to some of the points of difficulty. Many of the NDPBs sponsored by the Department have expressed concern at what they perceive as excessive interference by sponsoring divisions in the day-to-day running of their operations; this is seen as inconsistent with the separate existence of sponsored bodies. On the other side, the Department's concerns are to ensure propriety and value for money in the sums channelled through it by Parliament.

One possible solution to this set of problems could be sought in 'framework agreements'. That is, the Department could be assured that satisfactory processes, procedures, personnel, and monitoring were in place and concern for propriety and value for money could be met satisfactorily through specific framework documents, formal agreements and periodically agreed targets for the NDPB, without the need for day-to-day interventions. Agreed performance targets and the reporting of achievements against targets in formally documented procedures would be a central part of this type of approach were it to be adopted.

In brief, the corporate plan would have to contain an agreed 'mission statement' or objectives, and a series of agreed key indicators representing the outcomes expected of the programmes being pursued. Either the corporate plan or a subsidiary document would also have to have a set of agreed key indicators for administrative activities within the body. There would thus be a two stage process:

(a) agreement on the nature of the key indicators over a period (that of the corporate plan, say three to five years);

(b) agreement on the target values for the indicators for one or more years ahead.

Reporting mechanisms would vary between bodies but in one pattern key programme performance indicators would be part of the annual report, with annexes or separate documents showing administrative performance.

The implications of such an approach have yet to be worked out in precise detail but some initial thoughts warrant brief discussion:

(a) while general principles may apply to the NDPBs sponsored by the Department, the bodies are necessarily disparate and detailed sets of key indicators will reflect this;

(b) the way in which a NDPB structures its activities will both influence and, to a limited extent, be influenced by adopting an approach in which performance is represented by a series of key indicators;

(c) the idea that performance measurement is somehow peripheral to 'getting on with the job' can have no place in an approach which is based on an agreed detailed corporate plan and targets for a set of key indicators derived clearly from that plan;

(d) the pace at which individual NDPBs might be deemed to satisfy the standards required (in terms of structure, systems, personnel, agreed published corporate plans and agreed key indicators with targets) will clearly vary.

The implications for the Department in terms both of the structures necessary to adopt such an approach and measures to assess its own performance in sponsoring NDPBs have also yet to be fully worked out.

Conclusions

DOE has developed performance measures or indicators for a considerable proportion of its activities. However, the extent to which these can be seen as fully 'representative' of performance in the Department is not wholly clear.

In terms of administrative activities, the coverage of the Total Factor Productivity Index is substantial. Experience has shown that coverage and refinement increase as divisions become more familiar with performance measurement and its uses. On the programme expenditure front, the returns assembled for the purposes of the PES round have been improved considerably since their introduction. Nonetheless, problems remain with the evaluation of performance, especially as the degree of directness of control or influence on the part of the Department diminishes.

In this sense, the difficulties in determining appropriate measures of performance in respect of NDPBs exemplify the more general problems of the Department. NDPBs explicitly exist as bodies separate from the Department charged with specific responsibilities which are part of the Department's broader concern. Their performance is thus important to the Department, and the use of key performance indicators is seen as a central element through which the respective functions of DOE and NDPBs can be properly and efficiently assessed. But many questions about the best performance measures for the NDPBs, and the Department in its sponsorship role, remain to be resolved.

The need continuously to review and refine the approach to performance measurement in the light of these inherent difficulties is something which is doubtless common to many central government departments, and the public sector more generally.

References

Heigham, D., (1988), 'Public Sector Performance Assessment: Some Issues', in Beeton, D. (ed), *Performance Measurement: Getting the Concepts Right*, Public Finance Foundation, Discussion Paper 18, London.

HM Treasury, (1988), *Output and Performance Measurement in Central Government: Technical Guide*, Draft, London.

Housing Corporation, (1989), *Corporate Plan*, London.

Levitt, M. S., (1986), *Productivity in Central Government*, Public Finance Foundation Discussion Paper 4, London.

Levitt, M. S., and Joyce, M. A. S., (1987), *The Growth and Efficiency of Public Spending*, Cambridge University Press, Cambridge.

Molyneux, R., and Thompson, D., (1987), 'Nationalised Industry Performance: Still Third-Rate?', *Fiscal Studies*, Vol. 8, No. 1.

Smith, A. D., (1989), 'New Measures of British Service Outputs', *National Institute Economic Review*, Number 128, May.

Part III

The Future

Chapter 10

Performance Indicators, Root and Branch

Christopher Pollitt

Introduction

In Peter Sellers' last film, *Being There*, Sellers played the part of a simple-minded gardener who was eventually taken on as chief economic adviser to the President of the United States. His use of a few gardening metaphors proved politically more useful than the flood of technical economic advice which had hitherto deluged the President, not least because the latter felt that this was an independent, honest, yet reflective person in whom he could repose that most volatile cargo - political trust.

Faced with some of the technical difficulties of performance measurement there are times when most of us feel rather simple-minded. The overall purpose of the exercise can so easily sink behind the horizon as we become entangled in a dense undergrowth of particular measurement problems, massive data-processing requirements and clever but often essentially destructive criticism from professional service deliverers who are anxious lest performance measurement erode their discretion and autonomy. The aim here, therefore, will be to take a broad but sympathetic view of the growth of performance measurement over the last decade. Experts may continue to argue over whether the pruning is just right, or the foliage too thick or too sparse. The chief concern here will be the more general one of an amateur gardener - is the plant firmly rooted; is it the right shape; what does it need to survive a harsh winter?

No-one, surely, can complain at the rate of growth. The first major public service PI scheme was that for the NHS. It was launched in September 1983, with about 140 indicators per district health authority. From 1985 this became an annual event and both the reliability of the data and the method of presentation steadily improved. The foliage thickened year by year so that now the exercise generates ten times as many indicators as when it started.

Meanwhile PIs sprang up everywhere - the civil service, local government, the universities, the police, the courts. *Not* to have a set of indicators became the exception among the UK public services of the late 1980s. What is more, at least some of these systems were progressively linked to other important decision processes within their respective organisations, so that PIs became part of the normal way of life rather than hanging out on a limb as an unconnected, one-off exercise. In the NHS, for example, PIs were linked to the annual review process.

In the university world we have recently seen the allocation of a substantial portion of research funds according to an elaborate 'research selectivity exercise' which generated performance scores for every major subject, institution by institution, throughout the country (Pollitt, 1990a; *The Times Higher Education Supplement*, 1989).

Yet all in the garden is not lovely. Growth there has been, but of a lop-sided kind. Most indicators in most systems are still proxies for the first two of the 'three Es' (economy and efficiency). The third 'E' (effectiveness) and the proposed fourth (equity) are seldom captured, as was already noticeable in the mid 1980s, and the imbalance does not seem to have diminished much since (Pollitt, 1986a). When we look at the tree as a whole we can see that the major branches representing measures of effectiveness, equity, user-responsiveness and quality are all rather stunted.

When we dig a little, we soon find a second weakness. The roots of performance measurement, though slowly strengthening year by year, are still worryingly shallow. What little we know about the actual *use* of PIs within our public service organisations suggests that appreciation of their potential seldom extends down to the rank and file. Among service deliverers - doctors, nurses, teachers, lecturers, social workers, careers advisers etc. - they are frequently still seen as an imposition from above, as dangerously oversimplified, and as functioning primarily to provide senior management with a crude rationale for input minimisation (Pollitt, 1986b; 1989). Indeed, on occasion service deliverers have reacted with vigorous and sophisticated criticism of management-inspired PIs (for example, Skinner et al, 1988).

Barnes and Millar (1988), writing of PIs in the personal social services, accurately capture this sense of alienation from information systems which sometimes seem to have been created by the top, for the top:

'Those making inputs to the system do not always receive feedback in terms of outputs. Motivation to feed the system is low and the quality of input suffers as a result' (p2).

The roots are frail in another sense too. Partly because of the common feeling that PIs are somewhat alien entities, there is evidence that, outside the small circle who need to have regular recourse to them, actual understanding of the particular indicators in use is very limited. A CASPE team, researching the use of performance indicators in the NHS, found that 34 percent of their interviewees had difficulty in interpreting the standard boxplots (Jenkins et al., 1988, pp 129-136). Anyone who, during the autumn of 1989, has sat in on conversations in universities about the UGC's research selectivity indicators cannot have failed to encounter academics with inaccurate ideas about how those indicators were made up and what they should be taken to mean.

Patterns of Growth

Perhaps no special action is required to correct the weaknesses identified above. Official accounts sometimes make it sound as though improvement is simply a matter of time - with growing experience the deficiencies of these early systems will gradually be ironed out. Unfortunately, such teleological optimism is not wholly borne out by recent administrative history. If we look for examples of long-lived PI systems we find that development, stagnation or downright deterioration can occur, and that the balance between them seems to depend on an interaction of technical characteristics and contextual influences.

Two examples from overseas help illustrate this point. In the United States President Nixon's 1973 Federal Productivity Program generated upwards of 3000 performance indicators, some of which were still part of an annual Bureau of Labor Statistics exercise more than decade later (US Senate, 1984). In the mid 1980s this exercise embraced about 400 agencies, representing 62 per cent of the federal civilian workforce. By combining data on labour inputs, pay and labour outputs, the Bureau produced yearly productivity indicators. Between 1967 and 1982 for example, the system recorded an average annual productivity increase of 1.5 per cent. Given that the American political culture nurtures intense, if sporadic suspicions of government inefficiency (Pollitt, 1990b) one might have thought that this valuable time series would have been at the centre of political debate. In practice, however, it seems to have failed to attract much political attention, and also to have been neglected by many federal managers (General Accounting Office, 1983). Granted a few more resources and a higher political priority there seems no reason why the statistics could not have been considerably refined and their usefulness increased still further, but the necessary support has not been forthcoming (Levitt and Joyce, 1987, pp 54-57). This case confirms that the mere existence of a PI system is not enough to guarantee either its use or its improvement.

For our second example we may turn to the world leader in experience of public sector systems - the Soviet Union. For 40 years now its centrally-planned, largely non-market economy has depended on a shifting set of indicators to guide the managers of individual enterprises towards the targets hatched in Moscow. Here, surely, was a system in which the PIs enjoyed political clout. Perhaps, but the central politicians and planners were evidently unable to prevent 'gaming' from subverting the usefulness of the indicators as a steering mechanism. There seems to have been some kind of cycle in which, initially, the central planners would lay down a relatively modest number of simple indicators and related targets. Quite soon, however, the enterprise managers learned to 'play the system' by organising production in ways which satisfied the letter, but contradicted the spirit of the plans. Thus, where output targets were set in terms of weight, nail factories produced huge, heavy nails and the glass furnaces began to turn out impossibly thick sheet glass. At the 25th Party Congress in 1976 no less a person than President Brezhnev felt it necessary to condemn 'the chase after intermediate results'. As news of these mutations travelled back to Moscow the central planners responded by imposing more and more detailed, multi-dimensional targets, intending to reduce or eliminate the gaming (Nove, 1978). Unfortunately this eventually gave rise to a situation in which the rules of the 'game' were so complex and contradictory that few, either at the centre or in the enterprises, could fully understand or respond to them. At this point the system was ripe for the reformer who, in the name of simplification, would move in and reduce the number of indicators, thus giving the cycle a chance to begin again.

The moral of this case would appear to be that PI systems are potentially oscillatory - instead of steady improvement they may wobble between vulnerable simplicity and unintelligible complexity. Whilst it is true that IT now enables us to handle complexity more easily than could the USSR in the 1950s and 1960s, one still has to reckon with the limitations of the human analysts who receive the printouts. In our own NHS system the range of indicators facing each district health authority has grown from about 140 at the outset (1983) to ten times that number in 1989. If the CASPE researchers found a substantial proportion of staff had difficulty understanding the meaning of individual indicators, one wonders how many would be able properly to combine a number of indicators (the officially-recommended method for investigating key issues).

In sum, therefore, longer term influences may work against PIs as well as for them. At least two negative factors can be identified. First, political interest (perhaps never overwhelming in something as 'technical' as PIs) may move on, leaving the system without nourishment. Without political clout to spur management on, the system is unlikely to attract resources for improvement. Indeed it may lose the interest not only of the political leadership but also of the topmost officials, who can no longer afford the time to spend on a newly unfashionable issue.

Second, as in the Soviet case, 'gaming' may grow faster than those designing the system can cope with. Academics will chase citations rather than knowledge, school teachers pursue National Curriculum test results rather than 'education', health service managers seek high throughput figures rather than care or cure. To some extent - but only ever partially - this danger can be combated by more sophisticated indicators, but these may bring their own comprehension difficulties. It is an issue which probably cannot be 'solved', once and for all, but must rather be the subject of constant vigilance. Furthermore, it is a *behavioural* issue - a matter of how PIs are actually used in practice. As a quick re-reading of the present volume will indicate, this has not yet become the main focus of UK work on PIs.

The question for the gardener, then, is how these deformities and inadequacies of growth can be remedied. My suggestions in this regard are both technical and relational - in other words, believers in the potential of PIs must attend to organisational and political relationships just as much as to increasing the accuracy, relevance and timeliness of the data from which PIs are constructed. The tree needs some tender loving care as well as a better fertiliser.

More Branches

Of course there are well-recognised reasons why the development of indicators of effectiveness and quality have lagged behind those of economy and efficiency. The pre-existing data systems on which most first generation PI sets were founded did not encompass much if any information about effectiveness. That absence itself came about for at least two good reasons. First, collecting effectiveness data necessarily requires a measurement of impacts, and that in turn means going outside the organisation and trying to identify what those impacts are. Such expeditions are expensive and methodologically complex in a way that the accumulation of output data - lessons delivered, surgical procedures performed, etc. - is not. Second, for judgements about effectiveness to be made the impacts needed to be compared with the services' original objectives. But in a number of important cases these objectives had never been clearly defined, and certainly had not been ranked in a way that would permit a concentration of measurement on the most important dimensions of impact. This is at base a political issue: which (or whose) values are going to predominate? Is the NHS there to cure, to care or to prevent? Are schools supposed to prepare students for jobs, to enrich them culturally or to instill social self-discipline? Should prisons be assessed principally in terms of their custodial role or their rehabilitative effects? Should the police make public order their first objective, or the prevention of organised crime, or good community relations, or what?

At this point it is easy to despair and to retreat to the safety of input-output ratios. I would argue, however, that this would be unnecessarily, indeed dangerously, negative. To begin with, it *is* increasingly possible to measure *some* outcomes or good proxies. As Chapter 6 shows, in health care one can measure such things as perioperative deaths, unplanned readmissions, rates of nosocomial infection, immunisation take-up rates, and so on. Chapter 5 demonstrates that in education one can monitor the employment destinations of graduates, produce increasingly sophisticated bibliometric indicators of research publications and count the number of new patents or external grants associated with work in the technological and applied sciences. In the US particularly, but also in some Western European universities, interesting beginnings are being made in the measurement of the quality of teaching (Kogan, 1989; Pollitt, 1990a).

Of course it is easy to criticise the incompleteness of such indicators, and to stress the perverse incentives which may be created if too much weight is put upon them. But to be convincing, the analysis must surely always be comparative: how would decision making with such partial and tentative indicators of outcomes compare with our current decision-making without them? What are the perverse incentives which are built into our current, possibly highly impressionistic and unreliable decision criteria? In the United States interest in refining hospital mortality data took a great leap forwards *after* the publication in 1986 of crude and un-weighted data by the Health Care Financing Administration and California Medical Review Inc. The health care industry was outraged, but it also moved with great speed to see that more appropriate data, better contexted and explained would be used 'next time'. The moral of that episode is that resources and energy to improve outcome indicators come *from* an existing public debate about results rather than the other way round. If we wait until the measures are foolproof, we will never have the debate. Or, to put it slightly less controversially, even a few rough measures of outcome may be more valuable than yet more, and more precise, measures of process.

Thus far the discussion has proceeded as though the only kind of outcome data is of the 'objective' kind - mortality rates, employed graduates and so on. It is now time to question this assumption. For while this is the kind of outcome that first comes to the minds of many professionals, it is not necessarily the way in which the users of a service judge it. There may be a difference between 'technical effectiveness' (as defined by the experts) and 'consumer satisfaction'. Yet the latter is also a kind of outcome, and one of which many public services have until recently been fairly neglectful. What is more, it is a kind of outcome which it is often relatively easy to measure. Of late, therefore, various kinds of public authority have had increasing recourse to surveys of consumer opinion. For example, there can be hardly a District Health Authority that has not carried out some kind of patient survey during the last four years.

The 'consumer satisfaction' branch therefore is growing and is likely to grow further in the years ahead. But it would be easy to paint too rosy a picture. This far many surveys have been severely limited in terms of both scope and method. In the NHS their scope has frequently been limited to 'hotel' aspects (food-and-wallpaper) and has avoided the more politically sensitive issues of clinical care. And the method used has sometimes been a one-shot, amateurishly-designed questionnaire. Even the carefully put together CASPE patient satisfaction system at Blooms-bury - described in Chapter 6 above - has been criticised for severe methodological limitations (Carr-Hill et al, 1989a and 1989b; Crown et al, 1989).

Finally, there is a crucial logical objection to the play-it-safe strategy of sticking to 'objective' measures of economy and efficiency and avoid-ing the troublesome areas of outcome and quality. This objection is encapsulated in the question 'efficient at *what*?' Efficiency measures are valuable and necessary, but unless they are complemented by some monitoring of purposes and accomplishments one is left in a political and ethical desert. It may be efficient or economical to let the elderly die, to leave remote communities without certain major public services, or to use torture to extract information from suspects. These should not be the only tests of public policy.

Deeper Roots

In the present paper 'roots' are a metaphor for 'relationships'. The argument is that if PI systems are to thrive they will need not just one line of support (say, top-down pressure from ministers and senior officials) but several. Table 10.1 is intended to be a schematic aid to thinking about these multiple relationships. It shows four main 'actors'/groups in two locations. The groups are politicians, managers, professional service deliverers and the consumers or clients of public services. The two locations are the centre (Whitehall/ Westminster) and the periphery (local government, health authorities, police forces and so on). This is not a sophisticated taxonomy (for example, it does not yet include the important category of citizen/taxpayers who are not - currently at least - users of the service in question). However, it is already sufficient to allow some exploration of the different demands that different 'stakeholders' may try to make on a system of PIs.

Such differences between stakeholders may be classified in a variety of ways, one useful one is between:

(a) measuring performance as an activity aimed at renewing or reinforcing political and public legitimacy, and (consequently) as attracting political allocations of resources;

(b) measuring performance as a decision aid to management in adjusting organisational structures and processes, and internal resource allocation to support these;

(c) measuring performance in order to provide customers and clients with information on the quality, effectiveness, accessibility or efficiency of the services being provided (Kanter and Summers, 1987, p. 158).

The first of these purposes tends to be the particular concern of politicians and top management, the second of middle management and service providers, and the third of customers and clients. On the whole the present volume shows that the second purpose remains the dominant concern of

Table 10.1: UK Performance Indicator Systems: Actors and Their Interests

	Politicians	*Managers*	*Professionals*	*Customer-Clients*
C E N T R E	Interested in PI systems for 'defensive' and 'control' advantages. Seldom have command of 'technical' details. Interest tends to be episodic (around scandals or Parliamentary investigations). Central political 'clout' usually necessary to get PI systems launched. Tendency for focus to shift from one fashionable indicator (e.g. waiting lists) to another, and to focus on 'league table' comparisons rather than disaggregated longitudinal comparisons.	Twofold interest in PIs: (i) to enable them to control the periphery (ii) to give early warning of possible 'embarrassment' to central politicians. The first interest is fairly constant, the second more episodic. The first interest will also tend to emphasise efficiency and economy over effectiveness or quality, especially when (as with most public services) the latter are hard to conceptualise and to measure.	Professionals at the centre tend to be either advisers rather than service deliverers, or lobbyists working for professional 'peak associations' such as the BMA or NUT. As the former, professionals may behave rather like central senior managers, although they will tend to be more cautious about 'big stick' or compulsory uses of PIs. As lobbyists these reservations will be even more marked: forms of PI which reduce professional autonomy or expose professional performance to public view will be resisted.	Tend not to be strongly represented - in any direct way - at the centre. Indirect representation - through Parliament - is unlikely to be powerful with respect to PI systems. They are the kind of technical issue which seldom attracts much Parliamentary attention and does not sustain even those brief bursts or interest which do occur.
P E R I P H E R Y	Local political inputs are much more important for some public services (e.g. social services) than others (e.g. the NHS). Local politicians may resent centrally-inspired PI systems as an encroachment on local political judgement by central politicians and managers. Local political interest in PIs is - like central political interest - likely to be episodic and relatively shallow.	Continuing interest, especially in 'league table' comparisons which may be salient for resource allocation decisions within the locality. But where the league table is inter-local, peripheral managers will tend to emphasise uniqueness (incommensurability) of *their* locality. Likely to 'game' any given PI system to the advantage of their locality/agency.	More interested in quality and effectiveness indicators than resource use indicators. Resistant to indicators which appear to facilitate managerial control at the expense of professional autonomy. Tend to emphasise unique qualities of their clients and localities ('case mix') and therefore to be suspicious of national or regional 'league tables'. More convinced by longitudinal series.	Priority interests: service availability, effectiveness and quality. Not so interested in cost indicators, unless service makes cost-related charges. Interest from individuals tends to be episodic - when service is needed. Command of technical details not likely to be high; unless users are collectively organised and professionally advised.

the literature, with the first one (legitimacy) following some way behind and the third (delivered quality) a long way back.

If, however, our optimism concerning the development of user satisfaction measures is borne out, then the 'roots' may be considerably strengthened. For consumers represent a new actor - and a most important one - in the PI 'game'. Properly done, satisfaction monitoring can contribute not only to the stock of management information but also to a process of public education. The public - who have often been underquestioning in the past - can learn to think more analytically about their experiences in using schools, higher education, clinics, hospitals and government offices. Just filling in a single questionnaire may provoke more reflection than usual, while more discursive methods of obtaining opinions (random exit interviews, for example, or follow-up visits) may empower users to define their own dimensions of effectiveness, rather than simply to accept those of the professionals.

At the organisational (rather than the individual) level, satisfaction monitoring can be used by consumer bodies just as much as by the managers of public services. The National Consumer Council has already done sterling work in this area (NCC, 1987). There is no reason other than their undoubted shortage of resources why Community Health Councils cannot play an important quality monitoring role in the reformed NHS. And there are - or could be - bodies in the education world which could do something similar for schools following the 1988 Education Act. Indeed, the more successful the Government is in promoting internal competition in these two major services the more vital it will become for users to have their own organisations capable of independently monitoring changes in quality and dissatisfaction.

Finally I turn to perhaps the most important constituency of all - local middle managers and service providers. An alliance between local managers and professionals would probably provide the most durable base for the development of PIs (Pollitt, 1989). It would enable PI systems to survive the swings and roundabouts of political fashion and top management attention. The PIs would cease to be alien instruments, imposed from above, and become tools whose justification lay in their regular usefulness to the rank and file. It is here that developments in outcome and quality measurement take on still greater significance. For the kind of indicators professionals and local managers would find most interesting would be precisely those that dealt in impacts, cost-*effectiveness* (rather than efficiency) and user satisfaction. These would be sophisticated systems, with plenty of detail available and complex allowances for 'case mix' (be it in education, health care, social services or the police).

Local staff would be trained to use PIs as 'tin openers' rather than 'dials' (Carter, 1987) and would gain confidence as they realised their enhanced ability to out-argue any attempt by top management to misuse PIs for crude control purposes. In other words, with this second or third generation of PIs there would at last be 'ownership' of PI systems by those groups who actually generate the data from which the PIs are constituted - service providers and service users.

This is, of course, an optimistic vision. It may never come about. Yet we already know enough to make it a reality if we so choose. Encouraging the growth of effectiveness, equity and quality measurement is one requirement - and one that, technically at least, we can already begin to see how to meet. The second need is to broaden ownership of PI systems so that service providers, service users and local managers all get in on what was formerly a game played from the 'top' down and the 'centre' outwards. This will take time, training and resources. No doubt there will also need to be a struggle; shifts in organisational power relationships seldom take place without one. It is the suggestion of this paper that the chance of raising the performances of our major public services, and the near certainty of raising the level of debate about them, are prizes worth time and money - and a bit of a struggle.

References

Barnes, M., and Millar, N. (eds), (1988), 'Performance Measurement in Personal Social Services', Special Issue of *Research Policy and Planning*, 6.2.

Carr-Hill, R., Dixon, P., and Thompson, A., (1989a), 'Too Simple for Words', *Health Service Journal*, pp 728-729, 15 June.

Carr-Hill, R., Dixon, P., and Thompson, A., (1989b), 'Putting Patients Before the Machine', *Health Service Journal*, pp 1132-1133, 14 September.

Carter, N., (1987), *Performance Indicators: A Review of Concepts and Issues*, Mimeo, School of Humanities and Social Sciences, University of Bath.

Cave, M., Hanney, S., Kogan, M., and Trevett, G., (1988), *The Use of Performance Indicators in Higher Education: A Critical Analysis of Developing Practice*, Jessica Kingsley Publishers.

Crown, J., Harvey, J., Kerruish, A., and Wickens, I., (1989), 'Proof of the Pudding', *Health Service Journal*, pp 1070-1071, 31 August.

Department of Health and Social Security, (1988), *Comparing Health Authorities: Health Service Indicators 1983-1986*, London.

General Accounting Office, (1983), *Increased Use of Productivity Management Can Help Control Government Costs*, Washington DC, GAO.

Jenkins, L., Bardsley, M., Coles, J., Wickens, I., and Leow, H., (1987), *Use and Validity of NHS Performance Indicators - A National Survey*, London, CASPE Research.

Kanter, R. M., and Summers, D. V., (1987), 'Doing Well While Doing Good: Dilemmas of Performance Measurement in Non Profit Organisations and the Need for a Multiple-Constituency Approach', pp 154-166, in W. W. Powell (ed), *The Non Profit Sector: Research Handbook*, New Haven, Yale University Press.

Kogan, M., (ed), (1989), *Evaluating Higher Education*, London, Jessica Kingsley Publishers.

National Consumer Council, (1987), *Performance Measurement and the Consumer*, London.

Nove, A., (1978), *The Soviet Economic System*, London, Allen & Unwin.

Pollitt, C., (1986a), 'Beyond the Managerial Model: The Case for Broadening Performance Assessment in Government and the Public Services', *Financial Accountability and Management*, Vol. 2, No. 3, Autumn.

Pollitt, C., (1986b), 'Models of Policy Implementation: The Case of the NHS', *Teaching Politics*, Vol. 15, No. 3, September.

Pollitt, C., (1987), 'The Politics of Performance Assessment: Lessons for Higher Education?', *Studies in Higher Education*, Vol. 12, No. 1.

Pollitt, C., (1989), 'Performance Indicators in the Longer Term', *Public Money and Management*, 9.3, pp 51-55, Autumn.

Pollitt, C., (1990a), 'Measuring University Performance: Never Mind the Quality, Never Mind the Width', *Higher Education Quarterly*, 44:1, pp 58-79, Winter.

Pollitt, C., (1990b), *Managerialism and the Public Services: The Anglo-American Experience*, Blackwell, Oxford.

Rivlin, A., (1971), *Systematic Thinking for Social Action*, Washington DC, The Brookings Institution.

Skinner, P. W., Riley, D., and Thomas, E., (1988), 'Use and Abuse of Performance Indicators', *British Medical Journal*, 297, pp 1256-1259, November.

The Times Higher Education Supplement, (1989), No. 878, 1 September (various articles on UGC research selectivity exercise.

US Senate Committee on Governmental Affairs, (1984), *Management Theories in the Private and Public Sectors*, Senate Hearings 98-1218, Washington DC, US Government Printing Office.

Chapter 11

Some Concluding Observations

Martin Cave and Maurice Kogan

The New 'Evaluative State'

The developments described in this book reflect major shifts in the assumptions and practice of government. The trend at large, in the UK and in other Western European countries, has been christened the Rise of the Evaluative State. By this, Neave (1988) - taking higher education as an example - refers to policies that were first developed in part as an empirical, short-term response to financial difficulties at the start of the 1980s but which have now assumed a long-term strategic thrust.

The movement towards evaluation takes several forms. Some countries have established specific national agencies to review the performance of public institutions from above. Others involve the enforced strengthening of planning and evaluation at the lower levels of the system, which are then easily linked with evaluation and planning structures at the centre. Another strand identified by Neave is a shift from the analysis of input and process to that of product, by the creation of ever more elaborate criteria and performance measures.

The creation of the Evaluative State is by no means a systematic and consistently applied set of policies. It can, however, be thought of as occurring along two dimensions: first, the adoption of certain *a priori* assumptions about the nature of government which affect the modes and nature of evaluation, and, secondly, the institutional arrangements made to enforce those governmental objectives.

On the first dimension, the process has involved a persistent attempt by the British Government to secure more rationality - the matching of means to the pursuit of predetermined ends - in its policy making and implementation. The present Comptroller and Auditor-General has discerned three stages in this process: the period of 'rules'; the period of 'ethos and tradition'; and the period of 'calculation' (Bourn, 1989). In the last period, 'special emphasis is laid on setting objectives; determining the best mode of their achievement; and evaluating the economy, efficiency and effectiveness with which they are achieved'. The milestones along this route include the Financial Management Initiative (1982), the Next Steps Initiative (1988) and the publication of the Treasury's *Policy Evaluation: A Guide for Managers* (1988b) (see Chapter 4).

The effects of the change have been described (Henkel, forthcoming) as a substitution of the influence of service-oriented professionals by management criteria and expertise. A particular culture of management has been installed, first in central government, and then in other areas of the public sector, based upon economic concepts of rationality. 'Accountability was to be based on a model of rational man seeking to maximise his own individual interests in an economy aimed at the dominance of private over public expenditure.' In this dispensation, 'providers will be required to concentrate on maximising output from limited resources and an important aim of management will be to locate responsibility for performance on these criteria more precisely. Many of the government objectives were to depend for their achievement on effective review and control mechanisms. Economy, efficiency and effectiveness of performance had to be measured and compared between as well as within organisations' (ibid).

Throughout the 1980s the Government promoted evaluation most particularly to enhance central control over the agencies at the periphery. In so doing it exemplified a shift from the epistemological assumptions underlying the evaluative movements of the 1970s and early 1980s. According to Henkel, the earlier tradition, bred in the USA, relied on social science to solve and evaluate problems, whereas in the 1980s government wanted to leave as much as possible of that task to the market and to harness expertise to the management of public resources and to the reduction of the public sector: 'concepts of value in the public sector came to be resource-led rather than needs-led'.

Evaluation theorists struggled with competing objectives and methodologies. In the face of theoretical uncertainty and profusion two kinds of strategy were adopted. One was to eschew comprehensive evaluation and instead to direct attention to precise and limited objectives and audiences. A second strategy was to attempt to synthesise multiple evaluation methods and approaches.

The British Government felt no necessity to heed these complications, and, in fact, largely by-passed the debates about the modes and perils of different forms of evaluation. Those in authority determined to set clear objectives based on limited evaluative criteria. Where the market could not render judgements through prices and quantities bought and sold, other techniques such as inspection and audit could be applied.

The pursuit of this form of rationalism was to be achieved by the restructuring of public institutions for evaluation. The Audit Commission was created in 1982, and mandated to go beyond the audit function and promote local authority economy, efficiency, and effectiveness (see Chapter 7). Its background advice to auditors is based on special studies of local authorities who also receive their conclusions in a constant flow of publications. These contain the fruits of empirical work heavily enriched with prescriptions on how to move from dominance by Welfare State professionalism to a world in which clients are sovereign; the ways of the market rather than of public bureaucracies become the model. The National Audit Office was also given specific statutory responsibility under the National Audit Act of 1983 to move towards value for money investigations of the implementation of government policy.

Central government inspectorates increasingly directed themselves towards more determined monitoring in education and in the social services and the earlier intention to remain aloof from inspectorial evaluation, except in certain statutorily defined areas, was decisively abandoned.

These moves must be seen against a background in which, until quite recently, British Governments were somewhat reluctant practitioners of the arts of policy analysis of which programme evaluation forms a part (Gray and Jenkins, 1983; Williams, 1983). But since then evaluation seems to have taken off, particularly in its hard nosed and quantitative forms; as Christopher Pollitt observes in Chapter 10 above, there is now hardly a public sector domain that is not subject to performance measurement. Yet the overall picture is not that of a sustained and uniform approach to the issues; in fact, if we regard states as having clear boundaries and a minimum of common policies, what we observe is hardly an evaluative state.

In part the uncertainty and ambivalence reflect ambivalence about the value systems of which evaluative procedures are merely the observing eye. Thus one of the stated objectives of the Education Reform Act 1988 was to release schools and colleges from the alleged managerialism and politically inspired interference of local education authorities. But once emancipated by the provision of local management schemes, the schools would be subject to closer monitoring and evaluation by the very local education authorities from whom they were to be freed. One could ask what would happen to all of this additional and more sophisticated evaluation once it was completed, granted the weakening of the role of the local authorities. Perhaps the unstated intention is to create a shift from prescription, involving close control over resources, key appointments to schools and the like, to normative modes of influence in which more rigorous knowledge about performance becomes available to those who have authority to act, that is, the governors and central government. The local authority would from now on be acting with restricted powers to pursue default, but no more.

Thus the growth of evaluation in government can be characterised as being based on assumptions about the purposes and modes of government, and involving a decisive reshaping and development of evaluating institutions in which professional thinking gave space to managerial monitoring and criteria of efficacy. The rationality was not complete or internally consistent but powerful and pervasive nonetheless. This was particularly evident when legislation altered the relationship between central, local and institutional levels of government.

Agencies and Markets

Another facet of the centralisation/decentralisation issue is the link between output measurement and the implementation of schemes for decentralised management. Two modes of decentralisation are relevant here - the establishment of 'Next Steps' Agencies and the use of markets or quasi-markets to allocate resources.

The logic behind the establishment of Agencies is to divorce executive functions of Government from policy-making functions which will be assigned to Agencies run by managers with clear responsibilities and targets. When an Agency is set up, the responsible Minister and associated Department are viewed as its 'owner'; the Agency is managed with a greater degree of independence, but subject to accountability to Ministers and through them to Parliament. Chief Executives are thus personally accountable to their Ministers for the discharge of responsibilities set out in the Agency's framework document and for achievement of performance targets. Their pay will be related to performance.

It is clear that the Agency system places increased demands on output and performance measures, by establishing more transparent management objectives sustained by an incentive system for the Chief Executive. This is in addition to the requirements placed on performance measures by internal management needs within the Agency. Both internally and externally, the measures are being used to set targets, to monitor on-going performance and to analyse departures from agreed plans and targets. Inevitably, particular stress needs to be placed on measuring the quality of output.

If Agencies are successful, they will presumably be expected to produce either better quality output, or a reduction in running costs in excess of the standard target of 1.5% per annum, or both. The more decentralised framework of an Agency leaves open the question of how savings in excess of target are to be distributed between the Agency and its sponsors. This is likely to depend upon individual circumstances and a judgement about the source of the saving.

It is not yet clear how these arrangements are working out in practice as by March 1990 only 12 small agencies had been set up (a further 18 began operation in April, when it was announced that the arrangement would be extended to non-departmental public bodies). In principle, all agencies should have a set of performance indicators, based on an underlying business plan, at the start of their life. In practice, several of them have come into existence without an agreed set of performance targets. Given the increased role of such targets, there is clearly a risk in such delays.

The Agency framework gives extra impetus to develop what is broadly the same general framework of performance measures. It sharpens the need for, rather than changes the nature of such measures. A more fundamental change in their role comes about with the development of markets or quasi-markets in the public sector.

When a good or service is bought directly by its final user (the usual case) a full market is operating. Market failure may arise from monopolisation, externalities, information problems and so on, but the consumer or customer is usually able to make a quality judgement and exercise a choice. When buying decisions are made by an agent (normally a public sector agent) on behalf of clients to whom the service is then allocated directly, a quasi-market is in operation.

Such quasi-markets are emerging in a variety of different contexts, notably in local government, health and higher education. An early form was competitive tendering for such services as refuse collection or hospital cleaning. The scale of such competition increased markedly throughout the 1980s and often pitted private sector contractors against the incumbent public sector supplier. There have been substantial controversies about its effects, most of them hinging upon the relationship between cost saving and supposed deterioration in the quality of service.

The proposed introduction of 'internal markets' in the National Health Service provides a further major example. Under the new arrangements, health authorities will have the opportunity to trade with one another for the supply of health care services. Public (or private) producers will sell to an authority, acting as an agent for its patients.

A third example is the system of bidding for places in higher education already implemented by the Polytechnic and Colleges Funding Council (PCFC) and now being put into effect by the University Funding Council (UFC). In the former case, the bidding process covered only five per cent of resources for 1990/91, though this proportion may increase in subsequent years. In the case of the UFC, all student places are, in principle, open to competition from 1994/95, although the Council has undertaken not to impose excessive adjustments on institutions.

It is instructive to take the last case as an example of the requirements placed on performance measurement by the transition to a quasi-market. The revised process assigns many decisions taken previously wholly on judgmental grounds to the operation of market forces; if price were the only consideration in the bidding process, this transfer would be complete. Yet the question of quality comes even more to the fore in the presence of competitive bidding.

In a tendering process, the successful organisation is usually the one which has offered to supply the product at the lowest price. In a tendering process for higher education places, the winning institutions will thus be under pressure, especially if they have underbid through optimism or inaccurate cost data. To avoid insolvency, they may be tempted to lower quality of service. This is precisely the charge levied against competitive tendering in local authorities and health services. To prevent it, contracts must either be sufficiently tight and detailed to prevent quality degradation, or institutions must have a sufficient incentive, perhaps that of a long run relationship with the customer, not to exploit loopholes in the specification of quality.

It remains to be seen what the practical effects will be of bidding by institutions to supply higher education places. The results of the process of bidding for places in PCFC institutions show the Council seeking to incorporate a quality variable in the process (by discounting high quality bids by 10 per cent or 20 per cent - thus giving them a better chance of success). But it also shows a wide variation in bid prices: in some subject groups, the lower quartile of the range of prices bid was less than 75 per cent of the upper quartile, and less than half the mean funding level for all places (PCFC 1990). This suggests either that institutions exhibit a large dispersion of costs at the margin or that some successful bidders will be under great pressure to lower their costs, possibly at the expense of quality. Both Funding Councils are aware of the central importance of monitoring quality in an environment of competitive tendering but for reasons set out in Chapter 5 above, measuring teaching quality is a difficult task.

This illustration demonstrates that the use of market-based criteria and procedures in the public sector alters but does not diminish the need for performance measures. Markets sharpen personal and institutional incentives and competitive tendering places great pressure on successful competitors, especially when they have underbid, possibly through commercial inexperience.

The Future of Performance Measurement

We have already noted the apparent long-run and ubiquitous nature of the move towards new modes of public sector management based upon more explicit specification of objectives and measures of performance. The wider effects of such a shift will take a long period to reveal themselves, and it is too early to give a full evaluation of the changes.

It is possible, however, to identify a number of key pre-conditions for the new approaches to be successful. The first is the development of better techniques for output measurement. Much of the conceptual groundwork for this has now been laid, and those involved in setting targets and measuring outputs now have a clearer sense of relationship between inputs, processes, intermediate outputs and outcomes than was the case ten years ago. The language of the 'production model' of public sector organisations (set out in Chapters 5 and 6 above) has proved useful in clearing away much ambiguity and misunderstanding.

Much remains to be done in refining and testing techniques of analysis. Chapter 3 describes several of these, notably statistical cost analysis and the estimation of efficiency through data envelopment analysis. The Treasury's draft publication *Output and Performance Measurement in Central Government: Technical Guide* (1988a, under revision) both sets out an approach towards performance measurement and describes the quantitative techniques available. But the procedures need considerable further testing. Particular attention needs to be paid to cost allocation within public sector organisations, where recent development in the private sector - especially activity-based costing - still remain to be applied, and in the measurement of quality of output, where the health sector has led the way, as described in Chapter 6.

But a more fundamental precondition for successful implementation of performance measurement lies in the successful shift of attitudes and skills within the public sector. As several chapters have noted, the use of indicators by government departments runs counter to the dominant tradition in British public administration, which has been one of applying commonsensical rationality to judging, at the input stage, whether a scheme is likely to prove worthwhile, and then ensuring that expenditures are kept within reasonable and legal bounds. The lack of systematic concern with outputs was partly tied up with a reluctance to interfere with the discretion of professionals at work in the different zones of public activity, particularly those involving interpersonal and social services or areas where the nature of the activities was thought to be too difficult for the lay administrator to penetrate.

The various contributions to this book have made clear the philosophical and operational difficulties involved in applying indicators and have also given examples of their potential application. The more fundamental effects of using them have not been fully considered. The most important positive effect is to make explicit much that is implicit in management. In particular, British administrators have been coy about stating values and objectives to the point where accountability has been difficult to establish and any assay of achievement or of value for money has been difficult to undertake. Where measures can be realistically installed, performance will be more justly judged. Issues and outcomes can no longer be obfuscated by the display of political or administrative style.

The most serious negative result might be a displacement of objectives. Chapter 8 shows that when performance measurement in local authorities is directed to the achievement of certain objectives, effort is perhaps unwittingly transferred from other equally desirable objectives; similar phenomena can be found elsewhere. The solution is to seek as comprehensive a set of indicators as possible.

Performance measurement often requires that hitherto idiosyncratic criteria, often based on specific forms of professional expertise, be rendered into simple calculable units. In such circumstances judgements affecting the allocation of resources or salary awards and the like can be made by managers or staff officers outside the professional groups who lead services. Performance measurement thus reinforces increased corporate management at the expense of professional power and discretion. Techniques such as peer review can mitigate this effect.

The contributors to this book have sought to give an account both of the current state of academic research into performance measurement, and into current developments with central and local government. The various chapters show a mixed picture, with major advances in some areas and limited progress in others. As often happens, technical developments have outstripped the capacity of organisations to assimilate new management practices; and the long-term consequences - intended and unintended - of the latter still remain concealed. Thus while output and performance measurement is here to stay, its long-run effects are as yet unresolved.

References

Bourn, John, (1989), *Government Accounting Standards and Ethics: The British Experience*, Paper given at Seminar held by the Centre for Business and Public Sector Ethics, Cambridge, (mimeo).

Gray, Andrew, and Jenkins, Bill, (1983), *Policy Analysis and Evaluation in British Government*, Royal Institute of Public Administration.

Henkel, Mary, (forthcoming), *Government, Evaluation and Change*.

HM Treasury, (1988a), *Output and Performance Measurement in Central Government: Technical Guide*.

HM Treasury, (1988b), *Policy Evaluation: a Guide for Managers.* London.

Neave, Guy, (1988), 'On the Cultivation of Quality, Efficiency and Enterprise: An Overview of Recent Trends in Higher Education in Western Europe, 1986-1988', *European Journal of Education*, Vol. 23, No. 1/2.

Polytechnics and Colleges Funding Council, (March 1990), *Recurrent Funding and Equipment Allocations for the 1990s*.

Williams, Walter, (1983), 'British Policy Analysis: Some Preliminary Observations from the US', in Gray and Jenkins.

Index

Contributors

Michael Barrow is Lecturer in Economics at the University of Sussex.

David Burningham is Lecturer in Economics at Brunel University.

Martin Cave is Professor of Economics at Brunel University.

Peter Daffern is an Economic Adviser at the Department of the Environment.

Stephen Hanney is a research student in the Department of Government at Brunel University.

David Henderson-Stewart is Associate Director, Management Practice Directorate at the Audit Commission.

Peter Hennessy is Co-Director of the Institute of Contemporary History.

Jeff Jones is Head of the Operational Research Division, HM Treasury.

Maurice Kogan is Professor of Government and Social Administration at Brunel University.

Sue Lewis is a member of the Operational Research Division, HM Treasury.

Christoper Pollitt is Professor of Government at Brunel University.

Helen Roberts is a Health Policy Analyst at the King's Fund Institute.

Robert Smith is Director, Financial Management, Economics and Statistics at The Civil Service College.

Grahame Walshe is an Economic Adviser at the Department of Trade and Industry.